CLASSROOM MANAGEMENT FOR ELEMENTARY TEACHERS

W9-AMN-321

CLASSROOM MANAGEMENT FOR ELEMENTARY TEACHERS

CAROLYN M. EVERTSON
Instructional Systems, Inc., Vandervoort, Arkansas

EDMUND T. EMMER
Research and Development Center for Teacher Education, University of Texas at Austin

BARBARA S. CLEMENTS
Research and Development Center for Teacher Education, University of Texas at Austin

JULIE P. SANFORD
Research and Development Center for Teacher Education, University of Texas at Austin

MURRAY E. WORSHAM
Northeast Independent School District, San Antonio, Texas

PRENTICE-HALL, INC., Englewood Cliffs, New Jersey 07632

Library of Congress Cataloging in Publication Data
Main entry under title:

Classroom management for elementary teachers.

Bibliography: p. 163
Includes index.
1. Classroom management.   2.   Education, Elementary.
I.   Evertson, Carolyn, M.
LB3013.C528 1983   372.12   83-13844
ISBN 0-13-136135-X
ISBN 0-13-136127-9 (pbk.)

Editorial/production supervision
   and interior design: Kate Kelly
Cover design: Wanda Lubelska Design
Manufacturing buyer: Ron Chapman

© 1984 by Prentice-Hall, Inc., Englewood Cliffs, New Jersey 07632

Printed in the United States of America

10

ISBN 0-13-136135-X

ISBN 0-13-136127-9 {PBK}

Prentice-Hall International, Inc., *London*
Prentice-Hall of Australia Pty. Limited, *Sydney*
Editora Prentice-Hall do Brasil, Ltda., *Rio de Janeiro*
Prentice-Hall Canada Inc., *Toronto*
Prentice-Hall of India Private Limited, *New Delhi*
Prentice-Hall of Japan, Inc., *Tokyo*
Prentice-Hall of Southeast Asia Pte. Ltd., *Singapore*
Whitehall Books Limited, *Wellington, New Zealand*

CONTENTS

PREFACE

Good classroom management doesn't just happen. Smooth-running classrooms where students are highly involved in learning activities and that are free from disruption and chronic misbehavior do not happen accidentally. They exist because effective teachers have a very clear idea of the types of classroom conditions and student behaviors that provide good learning environments and because those teachers work very hard to produce such behaviors and conditions. This book describes what *you* can do to create a well-managed classroom. The process is described as teachers encounter it: first by planning in several key areas before the school year begins; then by implementing the plan and establishing good management at the beginning of the year; and finally by maintaining the management procedures throughout the year. We have tried to make the materials as useful and practical as possible by providing checklists to help organize your planning activities in key areas. Numerous case studies are also provided to illustrate how important concepts can be applied in classrooms. We hope you will find much here that is helpful as you plan and organize your own classroom.

Like all teachers, our own experiences have influenced our understanding of classrooms. However, much of our knowledge about classroom management has been derived from research in over 300 elementary and secondary classrooms. Most of these classes were observed at the beginning of and throughout the school year in order to identify management practices associated with high levels of student engagement in learning activities and low levels of disruptive behavior, two classroom conditions that contribute to good student achievement gains. The guidelines, suggestions, and case studies in this book are based on analyses of observations in classes taught by effective teachers identified in these classroom management studies. The research program was conducted over a five-year period at the Research and Development Center for Teacher Education, University of Texas, and it was supported by the National Institute of Education. Of course, the views expressed in this book are those of the authors and are not the official positions of the Center or of the Institute.

We would like to acknowledge a large debt of gratitude to the teachers who permitted us to observe in their classrooms. Without the base of reality they provided, this book would not exist. We are also grateful to the many observers, school administrators, and other researchers who both assisted and enlightened us. Finally, we are very grateful for the skills of Kitty Hays and Judy Camps, who typed this manuscript.

CLASSROOM MANAGEMENT FOR ELEMENTARY TEACHERS

CHAPTER ONE
ORGANIZING YOUR CLASSROOM AND SUPPLIES

Arranging the physical setting for teaching is a logical starting point for classroom management because it is a task that all teachers face before the school year begins. Many teachers find it easier to plan other aspects of classroom management after they have a clear idea of how the physical features of the classroom will be organized.

The number of things that must be considered in arranging the typical elementary school classroom is amazing! Of course there is furniture—the teacher's and the children's desks, bookcases, filing cabinets, chairs, and a table or two. In addition, there may be audiovisual equipment such as an overhead projector, tape recorder, record player, and television. Visual aids such as bulletin boards must be prepared; charts, globes, and maps must be displayed; and storage for materials must be provided. Finally there are the personal touches that teachers often bring to a classroom, perhaps plants, an aquarium, or animal cages for hamsters. When you arrange these physical features, you will need to make many decisions. Should desks be set out in rows? Where should your desk be located? Where will reading groups meet with you? What areas of the room will you use for presentations? How will you and the children obtain materials and supplies?

Reprinted by permission of Tribune Company Syndicate, Inc.

The decisions you make will have important consequences for the success of your instructional activities. For example, if areas for storing materials are poorly placed, bottlenecks may occur when children get supplies or return them, which could slow down the activities or waste time getting them started. The location for reading groups must be chosen carefully, or else you may have difficulty watching the rest of the class when meeting with a group of readers. The positioning of desks is important: because a poor arrangement may interfere with visibility of chalkboards or other instructional areas, increase distractions during instruction, or make it difficult for you and your students to move around the room.

This chapter will help you make these and other decisions about room arrangement, equipment, and basic supplies. Each component is described and guidelines and examples are given to help you plan. In addition, a checklist of room arrangement items is provided. Use it to organize your efforts in this important task and to be certain that your classroom is ready for the beginning of school.

FOUR KEYS TO GOOD ROOM ARRANGEMENT

Remember that the classroom is the workspace for both you and your students. It is not a very large area for containing up to thirty persons working for long periods of time—as much as seven hours in a day. Furthermore, you and your students will be engaging in a variety of activities and using different areas of the room. You will get good results if you arrange your room to permit orderly movement, keep distractions to a minimum, and make efficient use of available space. The following four keys will be helpful as guidelines for making decisions about your room's arrangement.

Keep High Traffic Areas Free of Congestion

High traffic areas include group work areas, pencil sharpener, trash can, water fountain, certain book shelves and storage areas, students' desks, and the teacher's desk. High traffic areas should be widely separated from each other, have plenty of space, and be easy to get to.

Be Sure Students Can Be Easily Seen by the Teacher

Careful monitoring of students is a major management task. Your success in monitoring will depend on your ability to see students at all times. Therefore, be sure there are clear lines of sight between instructional areas, your desk, students' desks, and all student work areas.

Keep Frequently Used Teaching Material and Student Supplies Readily Accessible

Easy access to and efficient storage of such materials and supplies will aid classroom management by allowing activities to begin and end promptly and by minimizing time spent getting ready and cleaning up.

Be Certain Students Can Easily See Instructional Presentations and Displays

Be sure that the seating arrangement will allow students to see the overhead projector screen or chalkboard without moving their chairs, turning their desks around, or craning their necks. Also, don't plan to make instructional presentations in a far corner of the room away from a substantial number of students. Such conditions do not encourage students to pay attention, and they make it more difficult for the teacher to keep all students involved in presentations and other whole-class activities.

Each of the above four keys will help produce good room arrangement. The specific components that will lead to this goal are described below. By attending to these areas you will address all of the important aspects of room arrangement. You can be confident that you will have designed a physical setting that is efficient and conducive to student involvement in work.

SUGGESTIONS FOR ARRANGING YOUR CLASSROOM

Wall and Ceiling Space

Wall space and bulletin boards provide areas to display student work, instructionally relevant material, decorative items, assignments, rules, schedules, a clock, and other items of interest. Ceiling space can also be used to hang mobiles, decorations, and student work. The following points should be considered when preparing these areas:

1. At the start of school, you should have at least the following displays for walls and chalkboards:

Class rules (to be discussed in Chapter Two)

A place for listing daily assignments

Some decorative display to catch your students' interest, such as a bulletin board with a "Welcome Back to School" motif, or a display that includes the names of each child in the room

2. Other displays that many teachers find useful include an example of the correct paper heading to be used in your class, and a content-relevant display, such as one highlighting a soon-to-be-taught topic.

3. You will probably want to cover large bulletin board areas with colored paper. This paper comes on large rolls and is often kept in the school office or a supply room. You can trim the bulletin boards with an edging or border of corrugated paper. If you can't find this item in your supply room, you can spend a few dollars for the materials at a school supply center or other store. You can also find books of bulletin board ideas for sale at such stores.

4. If you need ideas for decorating your room or for setting up displays, borrow some hints from other teachers. A look in some other rooms will probably give you several new ideas.

5. *Don't* spend a lot of time decorating your room. You will have many other more important things to do to get ready for the beginning of school. A few bare bulletin boards won't bother anybody. Leave one or two empty and add displays later or allow children to decorate a blank space for an art project or as part of a science or social studies unit. Also don't overdecorate. Wall space that is cluttered with detail can distract students and make a room seem smaller. Your room will seem small enough when your twenty-five to thirty students are in it.

Floor Space

Arrange your furniture and equipment so that you can easily observe students from all areas of the room in which you will work. Students should be able to see you, the overhead projector screen, the main chalkboard, and any other area that will be used for presentations to the whole class. Of course, you will have to adjust to whatever constraints exist in your assigned classroom. Common problems are a classroom that is too small or that has inadequate or poorly placed chalkboard space or electrical outlets. You should assess your space and determine whether any feasible changes in order to accommodate whatever constraints exist. For example, if the classroom is small, be sure to remove unnecessary student desks, other furniture, or equipment; if you have inadequate storage, perhaps you can locate an extra file or supply cabinet.

   A good starting point for your floor plan is to determine where you will conduct whole-class instruction. Examine the room and identify where you will stand or work when you address the entire class to conduct lessons or give instructions. You can usually identify this area of the room by the location of a large chalkboard or the overhead projector screen. This area should also have room for a table or desk where you can place items needed in presentations and an electrical outlet for the overhead projector. Once you have located this area, you are ready to begin planning floor space.

   As you read each item below, refer to Figure 1–1, which shows an example of a well-designed floor plan for an elementary school classroom. Note how each item has been addressed in this floor plan. Of course, this is just one of many possible alternatives. The location of desks, the small-group area, and other physical features of the classroom will depend on the size and shape of the room and how different parts of the room will be used.

   Arrangement of student desks.   Many different arrangements of student desks are possible, but be sure to arrange them so that all stu-

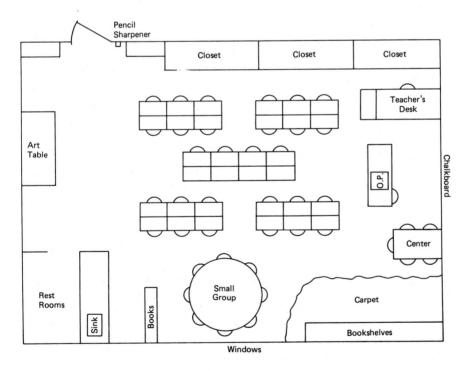

Figure 1--1   An Example of Good Room Arrangement

dents can look at the whole-group instruction area without having to get out of their seats, or sit with their back to the area. Even if other arrangements are to be used later in the year, you might want to start the year with desks in rows facing the major instructional area. Children are less likely to distract each other in such an arrangement than they are when their desks are arranged in groups with children facing one another. Note that in the classroom shown in Figure 1–1, the children's desks are arranged in clusters rather than rows; however, no child is seated with his or her back to the major instructional area; if the teacher puts a display on the overhead projector screen, all the children can see it by turning slightly in their seats and they can easily copy material from the screen onto their paper, at their desk.

It is important to keep high traffic areas clear, so don't put desks or other furniture in front of doors, water fountains, sinks, the pencil sharpener, or other traffic centers. Also, try to avoid having students face potential sources of distraction, such as windows, the small-group area, animals, or other eye-catching displays.

Be sure to leave enough room around student desks so that you can easily approach students to give them help during seatwork activities.

Some classrooms are equipped with tables and chairs for student seating instead of student desks. Table seating presents some special room arrangement problems, especially in grade levels higher than first and second grades. If students are seated on all sides of tables, some will have their backs to instructional presentation areas. If you have enough space and tables, this visibility problem can be avoided by seating students on only three sides of the tables. An additional problem that can be very troublesome is storage of students' supplies such as paper, notebooks, textbooks, crayons, and scissors. If there are no individual storage spaces under tables, tote trays (boxes or plastic dish tubs) may be used for students' materials. These must be stored on easily accessible shelves or carts. Plan the location of this storage area or areas carefully, for it will be used frequently and often by many students at once. Give thorough consideration to traffic patterns around and near tote-tray storage areas.

Count the desks or chairs and make sure you have enough. Replace damaged furniture or have it repaired.

Small-group area.   You will need an area where you can meet with small groups of children, usually for reading instruction, and sometimes for math and other small-group activities. This area should be arranged so that you can observe the rest of the class from your position within the small group. Thus your chair should be placed so that you face the whole class. Note the position of the small-group area in Figure 1–1. If you are seated facing out toward the room, you can monitor the whole class even when working with the small group. In contrast, if you were seated in the opposite chair with your back to the class, you could not see unless you turned around. Note also that there is a table in this small-group area. Although it is not required for a reading group, a table does allow this area to be used for small-group activities that include writing or working with materials.

When a table (or extra chairs) is not available, students may be asked to carry their chairs and place them in a circle (or to sit on a rug) for group instruction. An alternative to student movement is for the teacher to assign seats so that students can remain at their desks or tables for small-group instruction, while the teacher moves from group to group.

The teacher's desk, filing cabinet, overhead projector, and other equipment.   Your desk needs to be placed where it is functional. If you intend to use your desk to store instructional materials, then it should be adjacent to the whole-class instructional area and preferably near any other major instructional area. If you plan to work at your desk at any time during the day, you will need to position your desk to facilitate monitoring of students. Use the same principle here as with placing the small-group area: Sit facing the students and be sure you can observe all of them from your seat. It is not necessary that students be able to see *you* from their seats, and some teachers prefer placing their desks at the back of the room rather than the front. If you plan to work with individual students at your desk, you will have to consider traffic patterns near your desk. Student desks should not be so close that students would be distracted by individuals approaching your desk or working with you there. Other furniture items, such as the filing cabinet and storage cabinets, need to be located where they are functional. Seldom-used supplies can be safely tucked away in a corner or hidden out of view. Furniture that contains items that will be used frequently must be located near the area in which they will be used.

Bookcases.   Bookcases should be placed where they will neither prevent your monitoring nor obstruct students' ability to see chalkboards or relevant displays. If the bookcases contain items that will be used frequently, such as dictionaries or supplemental readers, then the bookcases need to be conveniently located and easily monitored. If a bookcase is being used to store seldom-used items, then an out-of-the-way place is best. If you have only one bookcase, try to store unneeded items in a cabinet so that the bookcase can be used for the necessary materials.

Centers.   A center is an area where students come to work on a special activity or to study some topic. Often a center will have special equipment, such as a tape recorder with headphones for individual students. Other centers may be built around a special study topic in sci-

"Come now, Miss Twist,
your class isn't *that* large!"

ence or social studies or around skill areas in a particular subject such as arithmetic or reading. In the last case the teacher might include a box of activity cards that students use to progress through a series of objectives as part of enrichment or remediation. It is important to note that you do not need to have a center in your room, particularly at the beginning of the school year. There will be time enough later to introduce this feature into a classroom if you desire. If and when you do use a center, be sure to place it where you can monitor students easily. Also be certain that all necessary materials and equipment (including electrical outlets, if needed) are available at the center and functioning properly. Plan a space to post instructions for equipment use.

Pets, plants, aquariums, and special items.   These can add a personal touch to a room as well as provide learning experiences for children. However, the first week of school is already quite exciting for students, so it is not necessary to introduce these special features immediately. When you do bring in such items, place them where they won't distract children, especially during whole-class activities. Of course, they should be placed where they will neither impede movement about the room nor interfere with work activities of individual students.

Storage Space and Supplies

Once you have decided on your wall and bulletin board displays and have organized space within the classroom, you can concentrate on obtaining supplies and providing for their storage. Some supplies will be used frequently and should be readily accessible. Other items will be seasonal or infrequently used and thus can go into deeper storage.

Textbooks and other instructional materials. You need to identify the textbooks and other materials that are available for use in your class. Determine which books the students are allowed to keep at their desks or take home and which must remain in the room for all students to use. Then find easily accessible shelves in a bookcase for those everyday books and materials that will not be kept in student desks. If you don't know what supplemental materials are available or what the school policies are regarding these items, check with the school principal, librarian, or another teacher.

Frequently used classroom materials. These are supplies that the children will use. Items included in a basic set are paper in varying sizes and colors, water-soluble markers, rulers, assorted pens and chalk for art projects, transparent tape and masking tape, stapler, and glue. These and any other supplies that are used daily should be kept at a readily accessible place, such as on a work table or shelves. Students are usually expected to supply certain materials such as pencils, erasers, pens, crayons, scissors, and notebook paper or tablets. Since you cannot count on all students bringing these materials at the beginning of the year, you should make sure you have an ample supply of these items. It is also a good idea to give parents a list of supplies that their children will need in your class.

Teacher's supplies. You will receive some materials from the school office for your own use. These items may include pencils and pens, paper, a large, lined display tablet, chalk and erasers, overhead transparency sheets, scissors, transparent tape, ruler, stapler, paper clips, and thumbtacks. In addition, you should have a grade book, a lesson plan book, and teacher's editions for all textbooks. These items can usually be stored in your desk.

Other materials. In addition to the items supplied by the school, a number of other supplies will come in handy. If your room does not have a clock and a calendar, obtain these now. Both should be large enough to be seen from all areas of the room. You may wish to buy a desk bell or a timer if you are going to use these as signals for starting or stopping activities. You should also add the following items: kleenex, rags or paper towels, soap, bandages, and extra lunch money for emergencies. Some teachers like to keep a few basic tools such as a hammer, pliers, and screwdriver in case a minor repair needs to be made. Store all of these items where they are accessible to you but not to your students.

Student belongings.   In addition to supplies that students store in their desks or in tote trays, you need to have storage available for items such as lunch boxes, outdoor clothing, lost-and-found items, and show-and-tell materials. Leave spaces for these items as you prepare your classroom. You might wish to prepare signs designating the use to which each space will be put. Planning for student storage will help keep your classroom from becoming cluttered and will help avoid the problem of misplaced belongings.

Equipment.   Check all equipment, including the overhead projector, record player, tape recorder, headphones, and pencil sharpener to make sure they are in working order. Get any necessary extension cords or adapter plugs and store these with the equipment or in a handy place.

Seasonal or infrequently used items.   This category includes Halloween, Thanksgiving, and Christmas items, and any other seasonal decorations, bulletin board displays, or special project materials. Also included are instructional materials that are used only on some occasions, for example, compasses and protractors, templates, special art project materials, and science equipment. Because you do not need to have ready access to these materials, you can store them at the back of closets, in boxes on top of cabinets, or even out of the room if you have access to outside storage space.

To organize and keep track of your activities as you arrange your room, and get your equipment and supplies ready, you will find it helpful to use Checklist 1 at the end of this chapter. Each aspect of room arrangement has been listed, and space has been provided for noting what has to be done and for checking off the area once you have it ready.

SUGGESTED ACTIVITIES

The activities described below will help you plan and organize your classroom space. Do as many of them as you have time for.

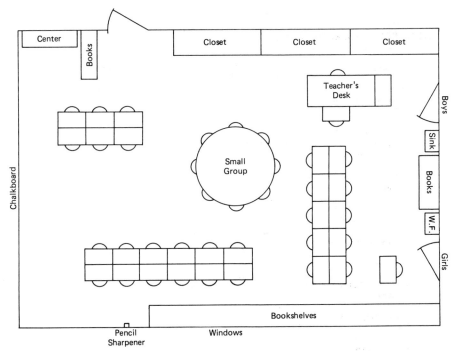

Figure 1–2. A Room Arrangement With Problems

1. The drawing in Figure 1–2 shows how one teacher arranged a classroom. There are quite a few problems with this room arrangement. See how many you can find and suggest one or more ways to correct each problem. (A key for this activity is provided in Appendix B.)

2. Make a scale drawing of your room, as in Figure 1–1. Use it to experiment with different furniture arrangements and the organization of space on paper, a much simpler task than pushing the furniture around yourself. Try to evaluate your arrangement using the four keys to successful room arrangement presented earlier in the chapter.

3. Visit some other teachers' classrooms and examine their room arrangements. Use the items in Checklist 1 and the four keys to room arrangement to guide your observation and analysis. If you are having a specific problem, ask several teachers for suggestions and look to see how they may have coped with a similar problem.

4. After you have arranged your furniture in your room, test the traffic patterns, keeping in mind the recommendations in this chapter.

(a) Taking the teacher's role, go to each instructional area and see if you can observe all students wherever they may be during the instructional activity that will take place in that portion of the room. Also be sure that needed materials are readily accessible.

(b) Now pretend you are a student in the class. Enter the room, go to several desks, check for visibility, for ease of movement to other parts of the room, and for possible distractions. If you discover problems, make changes.

CHECKLIST 1   Room Preparation

Subject	Check When Complete	Notes
A. Bulletin Boards and Walls		
B. Floor Space 1. Student desks/tables		
2. Small group area		
3. Teacher's desk and equipment		
4. Bookcases		
5. Centers		
6. Pets and plants area(s)		
C. Storage Space and Supplies		
1. Textbooks		
2. Frequently used instructional materials		
3. Teacher's supplies		
4. Other materials		
5. Student belongings		
6. Equipment		
7. Seasonal items		

CHAPTER TWO
CHOOSING RULES AND PROCEDURES

Good classroom management is based on children understanding the behaviors that are expected of them. A carefully planned system of rules and procedures makes it easier for you to communicate your expectations to your students, and it helps insure that the procedures you set up will be workable and appropriate. The goal of this chapter is to help you identify a good system of rules and procedures for your class.

Rules and procedures vary in different classrooms, but we do not find effectively managed classrooms operating without them. It is simply not possible for a teacher to conduct instruction or for children to work productively if they have no guidelines for how to behave, when to move about the room, and where to sit, or if they interrupt the teacher frequently and make whatever amount of noise pleases them. Furthermore, inefficient procedures and the absence of routines for such common aspects of classroom life as entering and leaving the room, turning in materials, participating in lessons, or checking work can waste large amounts of time and cause students' attention and interest to wane. A brief example of a classroom with major problems in the area of rules and procedures is presented below.

At 8 A.M. when the beginning-of-school bell rings, twenty-one of Ms. Smith's twenty-six fourth-grade students are in the classroom. Most are not at their desks but are milling about the room and talking noisily. Ms. Smith calls out above the din, "Everyone, sit down!" With much effort she succeeds in getting most of the children in their seats; however, three students are still standing and talking. The teacher goes to the front of the room and tries to begin a discussion of the previous day's field trip, but few children are listening. A few students straggle in at 8:06. Two others leave their seats. The teacher asks the children what they liked about their field trip. Only a few students respond. There is already some evidence of inattention: Several students are not facing the teacher, and others are quietly conversing among themselves. The teacher abandons the discussion and asks a girl to pass out some papers. At 8:09, students are sitting with nothing to do while the teacher talks with some children who have walked up to her desk. At 8:10 the teacher goes to the front of the class and announces that today she will show them something new. Two students are talking loudly, but the teacher ignores them. Three other students leave their seats: One goes to the drinking fountain, one to the pencil sharpener, and one to visit with another child. The teacher displays a definition on the overhead projector and tells students to copy it onto a piece of paper. Immediately, two students leave their seats to borrow paper, and the noise level in the room increases. About half the students get out paper. The students by the far wall are quiet, but they seem to be ignoring the teacher. One student goes to the closet, another to the pencil sharpener. Ms. Smith calls out, "Everyone, be quiet and get out some paper!" Several students call out, "What for?"

Observers of this classroom might criticize Ms. Smith for allowing students to get away with so much misbehavior. "Be stricter," they might say. "Punish the misbehaving students." Or, "Develop more interesting lessons to capture student interest." Some might even suggest that Ms. Smith set up a reward system to encourage good behavior. Although these suggestions could be helpful under some circumstances, they do not address the fundamental problem in this classroom: *The children have not learned the behaviors that are expected of them.* Furthermore, the teacher has not established procedures to guide student behavior. Problems are evident in several areas: the beginning-of-day routine, bringing materials for class, talking when the teacher is leading the class, out-of-seat behavior, attending to the teacher, and responding to questions.

Of course, even if the children know what is appropriate, they will not necessarily behave as they should. (For that reason this book will not end with the present chapter!) However, giving the children a clear set of expectations for what is appropriate will be a major start toward establishing a well-managed classroom environment.

Finally, keep in mind that the unique setting created by elementary school organization makes it essential to have a good set of classroom procedures. You will work with twenty-five to thirty students every day. Although your students will leave the room for lunch, recess, and perhaps some instruction, you will generally be confined to a single room with limited space and materials. You will be responsible for teaching many cognitive skills to a diverse population of students, and at the same time you will have to handle administrative tasks, arrange for appropriate materials and supplies, and evaluate students. In order to do these things well, you and your students need an orderly environment with minimal disruption and wasted time, leaving everyone free to concentrate on the critical tasks of learning. Carefully planned procedures help create this environment.

PRELIMINARY CONSIDERATIONS

Definition of Terms

Rules and *procedures* each refer to stated expectations regarding behavior. A rule identifies general expectations or standards for behavior. For example, the rule, "Respect other persons and their property," covers a large set of behaviors that should always be practiced. Rules frequently indicate unacceptable behavior as well as expected, appropriate behavior, although teachers sometimes manage to write rules that are only positively stated (for example, "You may talk when given permission"). In such instances the unacceptable behavior is implied ("Don't talk without permission"). In addition to general rules, many teachers will have a rule or two governing a specific behavior that could become an issue or that they want to prevent (for example, "Gum chewing is allowed," or "Gum chewing is not allowed").

Procedures also communicate expectations for behavior. They are usually applied in a *specific* activity, and they are usually directed at accomplishing something rather than prohibiting some behavior or defining a general standard. For example, you will set up procedures with your students for collecting assignments, turning in late work, participating in class discussions, using the bathroom, and so on. Some procedures (such as use of equipment at a center) are sufficiently complex or critical that you may want to post guidelines in addition to discussing them with the students. However, many procedures are not written because they are very simple or because their specificity and frequency of use allows students to learn them rapidly.

Identifying School Rules and Procedures

In most schools teachers are expected to enforce a set of school rules. It is to your advantage to do so. Rules applied consistently in all classes and areas of the building are easy for students to learn. The rules also acquire more legitimacy in the eyes of some students because the rules are *everyone's* rules. In addition to rules and procedures that regulate student behavior, all schools have certain administrative procedures that must be followed by every teacher (for example, keeping attendance records). You should know your school's rules and procedures before the year begins so that you can also incorporate them into your own classroom procedures. You can find out about school rules for students and administrative procedures for teachers at a school orientation meeting or from a teacher's handbook, a building administrator, or another teacher. Pay careful attention to the following:

1. Behaviors that are specifically forbidden (examples: running in the halls, bringing certain items to school) or required (being in possession of a hall permit when out of the classroom during class time, bringing a note for absence).

2. Consequences for rule violations. In particular, you need to note the responsibility you have for carrying out the consequence, such as reporting the

© **1968 by Bill Knowlton. Reprinted from** *Classroom Chuckles* **published by Scholastic Book Services, a Division of Scholastic, Inc., by permission of Bill Knowlton.**

student to the school office. If the school does not have a policy for dealing with certain rule violations, then you will need to decide how to handle them yourself.

3. Administrative procedures that must be handled during class time. These procedures include *beginning-of-year tasks* such as assigning textbooks to students, collecting fees, and checking the class roster. Money collection (for school lunches, for example) will go on all year, so you will need some system of record keeping and a safe place to keep the money. Some administrative tasks will have to be conducted each day. These include taking and recording class attendance in your grade book, handling previously absent students, and filing an attendance report with the office. You will also need a procedure for allowing students to leave the room to go to other parts of the building. Frequently, procedures in these areas will already be established and followed throughout the school. If uniform procedures have not been implemented in the school in some area, you may find it helpful to talk with experienced teachers about their procedures in the area.

Planning Your Classroom Rules

Once you have information about school rules and procedures, you will be ready to begin planning for your own classroom. Guidelines for rules will be presented separately from those for procedures.

Many different rules are possible, but a set of five to eight rules should be sufficient to cover most important areas of behavior. Five general rules that encompass many classroom behaviors are listed below. These or similar rules are often found in well-managed classrooms, although we do not intend that they be considered a definitive list. You may decide to use other rules (for example, a rule prohibiting a specific behavior) or different wording. Some teachers may find these rules too general, and they might prefer to have more rules with greater specificity. After each rule are some examples of behaviors related to the rule. When presenting general rules to students, it is important to discuss your specific expectations with students. When discussing the rules and related behaviors, it is best to emphasize the positive parts of the rules, rather than just their negative counterparts. When you do the former, you help students learn how to behave appropriately. You *will* need to be explicit about behaviors that are not acceptable when such behaviors might occur frequently (examples would be gum chewing, out of seat, call-outs). These may be incorporated into your set of rules or discussed when presenting procedures associated with specific activities. Be sure your presentation includes concrete examples and that you explain any terms that the children at your grade level might not understand.

The set of rules you choose will be used later in several ways. First, you will discuss these rules with your students on the first day or two of class. You will also post the rules in the room and/or make certain that students have their own copies. A posted set of rules allows you to focus student attention on and create a strong expectation about behaviors that are important to you. Finally, you may refer to specific rules as needed to remind students of appropriate behavior during the year. It should be noted that your posted rules need not (and cannot) cover all aspects of behavior in detail. Procedures for specific activities and perhaps some ad hoc rules will be needed. For instance, you may wish to post separately your policies regarding student work. Examples of some commonly used rules follow.

Rule 1. Be polite and helpful.   This may be worded in various ways (e.g., be considerate of others, be courteous). For the rule to have meaning, the children must be given examples: Listen carefully when the teacher or a student is speaking; behave properly for a substitute. Some "don'ts" include fighting, name calling, and bothering others.

Rule 2. Respect other people's property.   This rule may include guidelines such as (a) keep the room clean and neat; (b) pick up litter; (c) return borrowed property; (d) do not write on the desks; and (e) do not use another person's things without permission.

Rule 3. Don't interrupt the teacher or other students when they are speaking.   Use of this rule will prevent call-outs and other interruptions of lessons. You can use the discussion of this rule to teach the students how to comment or ask a question (e.g., raise a hand and wait to be called on).

Rule 4. Do not hit, shove, or hurt others.   Some clarification of what *hurting* means would be helpful. For example, will it include name calling? In spite of the fact that this rule is "obvious," prohibiting these behaviors strengthens the expectation that they are forbidden and serves notice that you will not tolerate them.

Rule 5. Obey all school rules.   This is a useful rule to include because it reminds students that school rules apply in your classroom as well as out of it. It also suggests that you will monitor their behavior in the areas covered by the school rules. Finally, including it in your rules gives you an opportunity to discuss whatever school rules are pertinent to your supervision of students outside of your classroom (such as on the playground or in the cafeteria).

Student Participation in Rule Setting

Some teachers involve children in rule setting in order to promote student "ownership" of the rules and to encourage them to take more responsibility for their own behavior. Student involvement can take many forms, such as a discussion focused on reasons for having rules and on clarifying the rationale for and the meaning of particular rules. A discussion might begin with a consideration of why rules are necessary. After this initial discussion, rules can be presented one at a time. The teacher may first clarify the rule by describing (or asking students to describe) the area of behavior it covers. Students can usually supply concrete examples, although they will tend to give negative instances, such as "Respecting property means not marking on desks or not stealing." Consequently, you should be prepared to state some positive examples. The discussion of individual rules may also include a rationale for those rules whose justification is not obvious.

Another way to involve students in rule setting is to allow them to share in the decision-making process for specific rules. This is sometimes done at a school level (mainly in the intermediate grades) by having student representatives from each room or grade level participate in the identification of school rules. However, within individual classrooms shared decision making is not very common for several possible reasons. First, the domain in which student participation is acceptable is limited. *Schoolwide* rules must be accepted as they are. Second, policies that are essential to managing instruction cannot be left to student discretion. Finally, elementary-age students may require considerable prompting to produce a comprehensive list of general rules. Thus, most teachers prefer to develop and present their rules, including students in a discussion of examples and rationales.

Another approach taken by some teachers is to limit student choice issues to particular activities or behaviors. For example, if gum chewing is not prohibited by a school rule and if you do not find it objectionable, then you could give your students a choice. It would be a rare class that decided to prohibit it! When students are given a choice, then you must also make them aware of their responsibility for making the chosen procedure or rule work and remind them they will lose the privilege if their behavior warrants it.

It is important to note that many effective managers do not provide for student choice in rule setting. Instead, they clearly present their rules and procedures to students and provide explanations of the need for them. A teacher who establishes reasonable rules and procedures, who provides an understandable rationale for them, and who enforces them consistently will find that the great majority of students are willing to abide by them.

PLANNING CLASSROOM PROCEDURES

If you have never analyzed the specific behaviors required of students in a typical elementary school classroom, you are going to be surprised by the complexity and detail in this section. Don't hurry through it, even though some of the items may appear trivial. These bits and pieces will combine to form the mosaic of your management system. Five categories of procedures are described: Procedures for room areas, for teacher-led instruction and seatwork activities, for small-group work, for transitions into and out of the room, and general procedures. A sixth area, dealing with keeping students accountable for work, is presented in Chapter Three.

As you read the items below, you can note ideas for procedures on Checklist 2.

Procedures for Room Use

Different areas of the room and furniture and equipment within the room need procedures to regulate their use.

Teacher's desk and storage areas.   The best procedure is that students may not remove anything from your desk or other storage areas without your permission.

Student desks and other student storage areas.   Just as students may not tamper with your desk, students may not bother the desk or storage space of another student. You can also help students learn good work habits by setting aside a few minutes each week for students to clean out and organize their desks and materials. This is a good end-of-day activity on Friday.

Storage for common materials.   Some commonly used supplies (scissors, scrap paper, rulers, etc.) and resources (supplementary books, basals, encyclopedia, dictionaries, etc.) will be stored on shelves, in drawers, or in cabinets. Most teachers label these storage areas appropriately and tell students at what times these materials may be used and whether permission is needed for any of them.

Drinking fountain, sink, pencil sharpener.   A common procedure is to allow use of these by only *one student at a time* and only when the teacher is not conducting a lesson or talking to the whole class. Some teachers require students to request permission to use the fountain or sink except during specified break times.

Bathrooms.   When bathrooms are immediately accessible from or adjacent to the classroom, many teachers allow students to use these facilities, one at a time, without asking permission whenever the teacher is not conducting instruction. A system should be established to let a student know if the bathroom is occupied (examples: a reversible sign on the door with a green light and a red light; knocking and waiting). It is also a good idea to go over bathroom use procedures, such as flush toilet, wash hands, wipe off sink area, and dispose of paper towels.

Centers, stations, and equipment areas.   Procedures that need to be established include when the area may be used (perhaps after other work is finished or during particular lessons only), whether special permission is needed, and how many may use the area at a time. Teachers often allow quiet talking in such areas as long as it does not disturb others. If talking will be allowed, then the area should be placed away from the rest of the class. Post rules or instructions for equipment use at each area.

Procedures During Seatwork and Teacher-led Activities

Good procedures for these activities are especially important because it is during these times that instruction and learning take place. Major concerns include keeping student attention, regulating participation, and providing assistance when needed. Good procedures will prevent or reduce interruptions or distractions that can slow down content development activities or interfere with student work.

Student attention during presentations.   It is important to consider how students should behave when you are presenting information to the class or while you are conducting a presentation or recitation. Typically, students are expected to face the teacher and listen attentively. In fact, teachers often translate this expectation into a general classroom rule such as "Listen carefully when the teacher or another student is talking." Teachers also expect students to remain seated at all times during presentations and not engage in social conversation, and to have only the books or other materials needed for the lesson on their desks.

Student participation.   You will need to identify some procedure to enable students to ask a question, contribute to a discussion, or receive help. During presentations and discussions, the simplest procedure is to require that students raise their hands, wait to be called on, and remain in their seats. In most circumstances it is not a good idea to allow students to call out answers or comments without raising their hands. Undesirable consequences of allowing call-outs include domination of participation by a few students, frequent inappropriate comments, and interruptions of discussions and presentations. Requiring that students raise their hands gives all students an opportunity to participate and allows you to call on students who do not have their hands up if you choose. Two exceptions to the "no call-out" procedure are sometimes permitted. The first occurs when teachers want students to provide a chorus response; that is, when they want a whole-class response to a question. This can be handled by telling students at the beginning of the activity that they do not need to raise their hands to respond. Also children can be taught a signal for a chorus response; cupping one hand behind an ear or giving a verbal signal, such as prefacing the question with "everyone" can be used. A second exception may occur during activities in which hand raising might slow down or interfere with a discussion. Again, students can be told that it is not necessary to raise hands during that particular activity. It is worth noting that the variations from the standard procedure of requiring raised hands usually should not be used early in the school year. Instead, follow a simple routine for several weeks until you are certain that students understand it. Then, if you choose to depart from the procedure, clearly communicate the difference to the students at the beginning of the activity.

Talk among students. Although student talk during teacher presentations is not allowed, some effective classroom managers allow quiet talking between students during seatwork activities when such talk is content related. Other good managers do not allow student talk during most language arts and arithmetic seatwork, although they may relax this rule during art projects or other activities when a little talking is not distracting. You will have to decide what your policy will be and communicate it to the students. The "No Talking" rule is easier to monitor, and you may want to start with this procedure during the first month or so of the school year. Then try allowing students to help each other on a trial basis. If you decide to allow students to talk to one another and to work together during seatwork activities, you will need to establish specific limitations. For example, you might tell students that during certain activities quiet talking is allowed, but if it gets too loud, the privilege will be lost. It would be best to demonstrate what "quiet talking" means and have students practice it to show you they know what is meant.

Obtaining help. When students are working at their seats and need help, you should have them raise their hands. It is not a good idea to allow them to call out or to come up to you whenever they wish. Once they have raised their hands, you may then go to them or have them come to you one at a time. Another procedure is to allow students to come up only if you are seated at your desk (or some other designated place) and not already helping another student. These procedures will eliminate long lines of chatty students around your desk. They will also allow you to control where you give individual assistance. If you choose to help students at a location other than their desks, choose one that allows you good visibility of the rest of the class.

Out-of-seat procedures. To eliminate unnecessary wandering around the room, you should indicate when students are allowed to leave their seats. For example, students may sharpen pencils, turn in papers, and get supplies only when necessary and you are not talking to the class. The "One at a Time" rule should be enforced.

When seatwork has been completed. Sometimes one or several students will finish their seatwork before the next scheduled activity. This situation is frequently handled either by having students complete an additional, enrichment assignment, or by allowing these students to use the remaining time for free reading or work at a center or to help with classroom maintenance chores. If you have enrichment activities that involve additional materials not in the students' possession, you will need to specify when these materials may be used, where they will be kept, and what the procedures are for returning the materials to the proper place. Note that if *many* students frequently complete their work early, it is evidence that assignments are insufficient or too much time is being allocated for seatwork activities.

Transitions Into and Out of the Room

Beginning the school day. You should establish a routine to open each class day. This routine should be supervised and led by you so that it is done efficiently and helps students "settle in" to the classroom. The routine need not be elaborate or time-consuming. Many teachers begin with social items such as a riddle for the day, a discussion of the day's lunch menu, the Pledge of Allegiance, date and birthdays, discussion of school events, or other items of interest. Not only does this routine establish a whole-class focus, it also gives the students a chance to get some of their chatter out of the way before beginning academic content activities. It also lets late students arrive before lessons begin or instructions for assignments are given. You may also wish to hand back graded papers or collect money, permission slips, or other items brought from home at this time.

Leaving the room. Your students will leave the room en masse at several times during the day: at recess and for lunch, physical education, music, or perhaps some other instruction. A common technique used is to have the children line up after appropriate materials have been put away, with the quietest table or row lining up first. Decide what behaviors are appropriate in line. Some teachers, particularly of younger children, find it necessary to specify where hands and feet should be while students are lined up. Some teachers have students clasp their hands behind their backs, others have students keep their hands at their sides. Line leaders can be helpful and students enjoy the privilege. Because noise would disturb other classes, talking is forbidden while the line is passing through the halls.

Returning to the room.   Frequently teachers establish a procedure for this transition, particularly after lunch time. A common one is as follows: Students are to enter the room quietly and take their seats; they may read or rest with their heads on their desks; students who need to use the bathroom, sink, pencil sharpener, or drinking fountain may do so, one at a time at each area. Note that this procedure gets students ready for afternoon activities. At times other than lunch, a common procedure is to return immediately to one's seat and stay there with no talking or perhaps whispering only until the teacher begins the next activity.

Ending the day.   A routine is needed at the end of the day to ensure that the students' desks and work areas are cleared off, materials to go home are ready, and students leave on time. Planning ahead for the end of the day guards against hurried closings, lost papers, and a feeling of confusion and chaos. Possible routines include feeding room pets, straightening bookshelves, tidying up desks, and stacking chairs on the desks. Other important end-of-day tasks include a short review of important things learned that day, foreshadowing coming events, and checking materials that will be taken home. If you have children who leave early to ride a bus, you may wish to do only the essentials with them and use the rest of the routine after they leave.

Procedures During Reading and Other Small-Group Activities

Getting the class ready for the activity.   Students must know what work they are going to do during the time they are not in the group. Therefore, you must post the seatwork assignments by group and discuss work requirements beforehand with the whole class. You should also note any materials that will be needed when the students come to the reading group.

Student movement into and out of the group.   These transitions need to be brief, quiet, and free from disruptions. Describe expected behavior to students: walk, no talking, hands off other students. You will need a signal to tell students when to come up to the group area. They should not automatically come when they see other students leave, because you may want to check on student progress before working with the next group. Some teachers use a bell or a kitchen timer, others just use a verbal signal.

Expected behavior of students in the group.   The rules for attention and hand raising used in the whole class can also be used in the small group.

Expected behavior of students not in the small group.   You will have given instructions to students not in the group and posted their seatwork assignments. However, students may need help as they work. It is *not* a good idea to allow students to come up to you while you are in the group; therefore, some procedure must be established to enable students to get help. One such procedure is to allow students to help each other. Another procedure used by some teachers is to assign certain students the job of monitors. Students can then raise their hands and the monitor can go to assist them. Permission to interrupt the teacher is then given only to the monitors and only when assistance is absolutely necessary. Often, students are told that they should skip the part of the assignment they are unable to do and that the teacher will help them later. You should check on student progress even while you are working with the group. Look up frequently to scan the class for signs of difficulty. Then when you change groups, circulate around the room to help students before you call the next group. Students can raise their hands between groups to indicate a need for help, or they may write their names on the chalkboard to signal a need for assistance when you are available.

General Procedures

Distributing materials.   At the beginning of the year books and supplies must be distributed to students. You will need some procedures for recording book numbers, noting damage, and handling some other details. These will be covered in Chapter Five along with other procedures for beginning the school year. In addition to the beginning-of-year materials distribution, you will have supplies, papers, and books to pass out every day. Unless you establish efficient procedures, a lot of time can be wasted doing this. Many teachers have student helpers pass out materials such as dittos, workbooks, or graded papers during opening activities. For the distribution of books or supplies, a student helper can be assigned to each table or row. If you collect papers from assignments by group or by row and preserve the order while you are checking them, you can then redistribute them to the class in the same way. This makes it easy to hand the materials to one student at each table or in each row.

Interruptions or delays.   If delays or interruptions occur while students are working, they should be taught to continue their work silently. Tell students that they should be courteous and patient if you are interrupted in the middle of a lesson by a visitor or a phone call and that you will return to them as quickly as possible. If you will be detained very long, give the students something to do.

Bathrooms.   If bathrooms are located away from your classroom, a hall-pass system may be established to monitor the number of students out of the room and to let students know if they may leave. You might hang a bathroom hall pass next to the hall door to be placed by the student around his or her neck or carried enroute to the bathroom. There may already be a schoolwide procedure, so be certain you know what it is.

Library, resource room, school office.   When one or a small group of students must go to another area in the school, you will generally remain in the classroom with the rest of the students. Schoolwide procedures are usually established to handle these situations. Find out whether a hall permit system or some other procedure is used to regulate movement of students in the halls. Also review any school rules that govern behavior in transit or at the locations. You will want to make sure your students understand these procedures.

Cafeteria.   Review the school policies for the cafeteria and be ready to explain them to your class before they go to lunch and after they return if needed. If you are planning to (or must) sit with the students, decide ahead of time who will get to sit by you and whether this will be at random, a privilege, or whether you will use assigned seats. If your students are too noisy or misbehave, you may wish to establish a reward system for good behavior or include lunchroom behavior as part of your in-class reward system.

Playground.   Safety rules are a must, and you should limit overly aggressive behavior and dangerous play. Also if any of the equipment in the playground poses a potential hazard, you will need to talk about it with your students. Make clear to your students what part of the school grounds they may use for recess. You also should establish some signal for getting students' attention when it is time for them to line up and return to the classroom; this could be a whistle or a raised hand. If you plan to play a game on the playground, announce this prior to leaving the room, telling students where they should go once out on the playground.

Fire and disaster drills.   You need to find out what school policies and routines have been established to protect the children and you. While you may wish to wait a while before teaching these to your students, you should not wait until you know a drill is imminent. It is better to go over these procedures ahead of time and then review them just prior to the first drill.

Classroom helpers.   Teachers often use students to help with such chores as erasing the chalkboard, passing out materials and supplies, carrying messages to the office, watering the plants, and feeding the animals. Students are often chosen to be line leaders and classroom monitors. Some teachers use these activities as privileges or rewards for especially good or improved behavior. Some teachers have a chart or bulletin board with slots for the names of students currently serving as monitors or helpers. A card is then made for each child with his or her name and this card is placed in the appropriate slot when that child has a particular room helper responsibility. Some teachers ask for volunteers for each job; others appoint students on a rotating basis or use jobs as rewards. Appointment is usually done at the beginning of the week and the appointments last one or two weeks.

SUGGESTED ACTIVITIES

1. Identify the schoolwide rules and procedures that you and your students are expected to observe. Be sure these are incorporated into your own classroom rules and procedures where appropriate.

2. Read the case studies on the following pages. They illustrate classroom procedures and rules for most major areas, and they will help you develop your own system of management.

3. Use Checklist 2 at the end of the chapter to help organize your planning of classroom procedures. Be sure to think through your expectations for student behavior in each of the general areas and the instructional areas that you will be using. Then develop a set of procedures that will communicate your expectations to your students.

4. If you have trouble developing procedures in some area or are not sure if the ones you have identified will work, be sure to ask other teachers for their opinions. They will usually be more than happy to share some of their "tricks of the trade."

5. Develop a list of five to eight general classroom rules. Be sure these emphasize areas of classroom behavior that are important to you and to the functioning of your classroom.

6. After you have developed a set of rules, review them with an administrator or another teacher.

CHECKLIST 2   Classroom Procedures

Subject	Procedures or Expectations
I. Room Use A. Teacher's desk and storage areas B. Student desks and storage areas C. Storage for common materials D. Drinking fountains, sink, pencil sharpener E. Bathrooms F. Center, station, or equipment areas	
II. Seatwork and Teacher-led Instruction A. Student attention during presentations B. Student participation C. Talk among students D. Obtaining help E. Out-of-seat procedures during seatwork F. When seatwork has been completed	
III. Transitions Into and Out of the Room A. Beginning the school day B. Leaving the room C. Returning to the room D. Ending the day	
IV. Procedures During Reading or Other Groups A. Getting the class ready B. Student movement C. Expected behavior in the group D. Expected behavior of students out of group	
V. General Procedures A. Distributing materials B. Interruptions C. Bathrooms D. Library, resource room, school office E. Cafeteria F. Playground G. Fire and disaster drills H. Classroom helpers	

CASE STUDY 2–1:
CLASSROOM PROCEDURES AND RULES
IN A SECOND GRADE CLASS

Ms. Able's students followed four rules: We are quiet in the classroom. We do our best work. We are polite and helpful. We follow all school rules. Students were taught that being quiet in the classroom meant that they usually had a choice of being silent or talking in whisper voices. When the teacher was addressing the class or when she told the class to be silent, students were to stop their whispers and be silent. Most of the time, however, students were allowed to work together, whispering. If a student was loud, the student lost the whisper privilege and had to be silent.

The rule "We do our best work" included listening carefully when the teacher was giving instructions, completing all assignments, turning in neat work, and making good use of time in class.

Student behaviors relating to the rule "We are polite and helpful" included taking turns in class and raising hands to receive permission to talk. Ms. Able explained to her students that in order for everyone to have a chance to talk and to be heard, they should raise their hands and wait to be called on when they wanted to answer a question or make a comment. Other aspects of consideration and respect for fellow students, the teacher, and other adults in the school were also included under this rule. In addition, the school rules referred to in the fourth classroom rule governed student behavior in the halls, cafeteria, and other common areas of the school grounds.

Several other important classroom procedures provided guidelines for student behavior in Ms. Able's classroom. Students were expected to stay seated at their desks whenever the teacher was presenting directions or instruction to the class as a whole. At other times, however, Ms. Able's students were allowed to leave their desks to get supplies, hand in papers, sharpen their pencils, and use the restroom that was adjacent to the classroom without asking the teacher's permission as long as they did not disturb other students. For example, students were allowed to sharpen a pencil without permission except when the teacher was talking to the class or when another student was addressing the class. No more than two students were allowed at the pencil sharpener at one time, one sharpening and one waiting. When the teacher was working with a small group or helping an individual, students were not allowed to walk up to her or interrupt. They stayed at their desks and raised their hands to request assistance. If students finished their work early, they were allowed to read their library books, work a dittoed puzzle, or play an instructional game. They could talk, using their whisper voices, but they could not disturb anyone still working on the assignment. Unless they had permission to do otherwise, they were expected to stay at their own desks.

When Ms. Able needed to get the attention of the class, she routinely used a bell as a signal. She taught students that when she rang the bell *once* they were to immediately be silent and look at her. She explained to the class that using the bell was a shortcut to save time, that she would ring the bell only once and not several times, and that she expected students to respond immediately. She used the bell in a very consistent manner.

CASE STUDY 2–2:
SMALL-GROUP PROCEDURES

At the end of the second week of school, Ms. Bernal announced to her fourth-grade class that they would be doing two new things that day: working independently and reading in small groups. She defined the word *independently* as doing their own work without interrupting other students. She then called students' attention to a group of exercises on the front board. These were spelling and language arts activities that the teacher knew students could do on their own. She gave directions for each exercise, step by step, doing the first of each type of activity as an example. She questioned students to be sure they understood what to do and gave them ample time and encouragement to ask questions. The teacher reemphasized that they were to work independently and told them that now was their last opportunity to ask questions before their reading group met. She told students to skip an exercise if they could not do it and go back to it after they received help.

Ms. Bernal then reminded the class that students could go to the bathroom one at a time, except when she was talking to the whole class. She announced that while she was working with reading groups that day, students not in the reading group could use the bathroom, wash hands, sharpen one pencil, or get a drink of water if necessary while they were doing seatwork. She then asked if there were any questions. There were none. She asked one child to repeat to the class what they were to do when not in a small reading group.

Ms. Bernal called out the names of the Green group members, then had them raise their hands. Then she did the same with the Yellow group and the Red group. She pointed to a small bulletin board where the names of the students in each group were posted below the group's color name. The groups would be called in the order on the bulletin board: Red, Yellow, then Green. The signal to come to group would be the timer bell. Each group would last about twenty minutes. Students were told to stack their books and papers quickly and neatly on their desks when they were called to reading group. They did not have to bring any materials to the reading group because the teacher would provide the things they would need. Ms. Bernal stressed that she expected the students to be very quiet coming to and leaving the reading circle, so as not to disturb students working at their desks. She told the class that she was very interested in hearing every student read, and this would be impossible if there were a lot of talking and noise.

Ms. Bernal then told the children that if they finished their seatwork, they were to take out library books and read quietly. She asked if there were any questions. When there were none, she asked the Red group (who were the slower readers) to come to the reading circle and told the rest of the students to go to work on the board work. The Red group moved quickly to the reading circle as the teacher waited and watched them and the rest of the class. The teacher's chair was placed in the reading circle so that she could monitor the entire class while she was teaching the small group. Once she noticed three students talking at their seats. She stopped work in the small group to remind the class briefly that she wanted complete silence during reading group and that she was watching for students who were particularly good at following directions. Later during reading group, several students raised their hands and looked toward the teacher. She noticed the hands, caught the students' eyes, and shook her head. This was a signal to these students that it was inappropriate to ask questions while the teacher was in reading group.

When the Red group's time was almost up, the teacher reminded them of her instructions about what they were to do at their desks and told them that she would check over their work after finishing with the second group, the Yellow group. With that she sent Red group to their seats and rang the timer bell. She watched as students in the Yellow group left their desks and came to the reading circle while the Red group began seatwork. She complimented the students in the Yellow reading group for walking quietly and leaving their books stacked neatly. She answered their seatwork questions before proceeding with the rest of the morning's reading activities.

Later during the year, Ms. Bernal introduced new activities in the reading group routine, such as listening center activities or language skill box exercises. Groups rotated from seatwork to reading group to some other activity. Each change in class routine was carefully planned and explained to the students so that they were able to participate in the activities in an orderly way as Ms. Bernal conducted reading instruction in the small groups.

CHAPTER THREE
MANAGING STUDENT WORK

When we presented a set of procedures for establishing an orderly classroom setting in Chapter Two, we also indicated that additional procedures would be needed to keep students accountable for their work. In this chapter we will describe the additional procedures, which are aimed at encouraging students to complete assignments and to engage in other learning activities.

Each day of the school year you will give your students assignments that they will be expected to complete in the classroom or at home. These assignments are important for learning and retention because they provide systematic practice, the application of knowledge, and repeated exposure to content. Thus, the consistent and accurate completion of assignments is a critical goal for effective management. If students are not held accountable for their work, many problems in this area can occur. Consider the following example:

> During the second month of school, Mr. Paul begins to notice several disturbing signs of a lack of interest in assignments on the part of a number of his fourth-grade students. This is most evident during reading groups and in math.

When Mr. Paul meets with reading groups in the morning, he usually gives students who are not in the group two assignments to do as seatwork. Generally one of these is a worksheet activity related to the reading assignment and the other is a language arts activity such as spelling practice or handwriting. Early in the year, Mr. Paul had much trouble with interruptions during the reading group as students left their seats and came up for directions and help. He put a stop to that by enforcing a rule prohibiting "come ups," but now students are talking constantly during seatwork. When Mr. Paul checks on their progress at the completion of reading group time, as many as half the students have hardly begun their assignments or are doing them carelessly and incorrectly.

In math after a presentation of the material for the day, Mr. Paul usually gives an assignment. If students do not complete the work in class, then they are expected to take it home and complete it there. Mr. Paul usually lets students check their own work, and he picks up work and grades it about once a week. During the last several of these weekly checks, he has discovered that four or five students are not doing the assignment and at least as many have incomplete papers with many errors.

It is apparent that many of Mr. Paul's students do not feel very accountable for their work. It is possible, of course, that some of the assignments are too difficult, but it is also very likely that many of Mr. Paul's procedures are not helping the students develop good work habits or learn the importance of prompt and accurate completion of assignments. The basis for the poor student effort could be determined from answers to the following questions:

> Are the required standards for quality and amount of work clear to the students?
>
> Is student progress being monitored closely?
>
> What kinds of feedback do students receive about their progress as well as about their completed work? How immediate is the feedback?
>
> What are the consequences for incomplete or careless student work?

Important areas of accountability are addressed by these questions, and in each area Mr. Paul could do several things to encourge students to complete assignments promptly and correctly. This chapter will focus on aspects of classroom procedures that communicate the importance of work assignments, that enable students to understand what is expected of them, and that help them make good progress. The critical areas include communicating assignments and work requirements, monitoring student progress, and providing feedback. Checklist 3 is provided to help organize your planning in these areas. In addition, three case studies of accountability systems of elementary teachers are provided at the end of the chapter.

CLEAR COMMUNICATION OF ASSIGNMENTS AND WORK REQUIREMENTS

Students need a clear idea of what their assignments are and what is expected of them. This means that you must be able to explain all requirements and features of the assignments. Verbal explanation alone will not be sufficient, because not all students listen carefully, some students may be absent when the assignments and requirements are discussed, and the assignment itself may be complex. In addition, there is more to completing assignments than doing the work accurately. You must also consider standards for neatness, legibility, and form. While we do not want to encourage an overemphasis on form to the detriment of the content objectives, some standards in these areas must be set. The following three areas should be considered.

Instructions for Assignments

In addition to telling the students what the assignment is, you should post the assignment and important instructions on a chalkboard. It is also a good idea to teach students to copy the assignment into their notebooks or on the first line of their papers so they will have a record of it if they need it to complete work at home. Go over instructions orally with the class, indicating where they are written on the board. Whenever possible, use the overhead projector or the chalkboard to *show* students what their papers should look like. After giving instructions, question the children and ask them to give examples so you can determine whether they understand what to do.

If you are giving directions for seatwork to several groups in preparation for reading group time, be sure the assignment for each group is clearly labeled. For primary grades especially, you might assign a color to each reading group. Then use that color chalk to put asterisks beside assignments or worksheets taped to the board to indicate the appropriate group, or write the whole set of assignments and instructions in that color.

Standards for Form, Neatness, and Due Dates

Before the children start, let them know what paper to write on, what heading to use, whether or not to write on the back of the paper, whether or not to color any part of it, how to number, whether to use pen or pencil, and whether to erase errors or to draw lines through them. You should develop a standard set of instructions for work requirements. Students will then learn what is generally expected, and you will not have to explain this to them each time.

Due dates should be reasonable and clear; exceptions should not be made without good cause. Be sure to tell students your policy for turning in work on time, and follow it consistently. Don't keep extending time limits; if you do, children may learn to dawdle to avoid work. Insist that work not done on time be completed at home or after school. This assumes, of course, that students possess the necessary knowledge or skills to do the work.

Finally, decide on a heading for students to use on their papers. Post a sample heading and go over it with students the first time they are to use it. Remind them of it several times during the early weeks of school until they use it properly.

Procedures for Absent Students

A number of problems arise when students are absent. They miss instruction, directions for assignments, and assistance they may need in getting work underway. Establishing some routines for handling makeup work can be very helpful to these students. You may not require that students complete each assignment that they missed while they were absent, but a student who misses critical assignments will need to make these up. The following items should be considered.

1. Arrange to meet briefly with the student who has been absent. Let him or her know what makeup work is required. If you post weekly assignment lists for each subject on a bulletin board or keep a folder with lists of assignments in an easily accessible place, you will be able to point out which of these are to be completed. Be sure to let the student know how much time is allowed for makeup work.

2. Designate a place where students can turn in makeup work and where they can pick it up after it has been checked (for example, baskets or trays labeled "Absent In" and "Absent Out").

3. Establish a regular time, such as fifteen minutes before or after school, when you will be available to assist students with makeup work. In addition, you can designate class helpers who will be available at particular times of the day (usually during seatwork activities) to help these students.

MONITORING PROGRESS ON AND COMPLETION OF ASSIGNMENTS

Monitoring Work in Progress

Monitoring student progress helps you detect students who are having difficulty and also allows you to encourage other students to keep working. Once you have made an assignment, you should give careful attention to student work. Don't immediately begin work at your desk or go to help an individual student without checking to see if all students are

"It's one of my better sales talks on reasons for
completing homework on time!"

starting work and are able to do the assignment. If you don't check some students won't even start the assignment and others may begin it incorrectly. Two simple strategies can help to avoid this situation. First, if everyone in the class is doing the same assignment you can assure a smooth transition into seatwork by beginning it as a whole class activity; that is, have everyone get out their paper worksheet, or other materials and then answer the first question or two or work the first few problems together as a group just as you would conduct a recitation. For example, ask the first question, solicit an answer, discuss it, and have students record it on their paper. Not only will this procedure ensure that all students begin working, but any immediate problems with the assignment can be solved. A second way to monitor student involvement in the assignment is to circulate around the room and check each student's progress periodically. This allows corrective feedback to be given when needed and helps keep students responsible for appropriate progress. Note the progress of all students not just those who raise their hands for help. Another way to monitor work in progress is to have students bring their work to you one at a time at some designated point in the activity.

If you are working with reading groups and some students are doing seatwork while you are meeting with the group, don't wait until the end of the reading period to check student progress on seatwork. Go around to the students between meeting with reading groups to be sure the students are doing the work correctly.

Sometimes assignments are given that are not due for several days or even a week or longer. Examples include notebooks, reports, and science or social studies projects. When this is the case you will need to be especially careful to monitor student progress. Define sub-stages in the project or assignment, then set deadlines and goals for each of these parts. This will help students organize their work and make it easier for you to evaluate their progress.

Monitoring the Completion of Assignments

Monitoring completion of assignments has several components. First, you will need to establish regular procedures for students to turn in completed work and for you to note whose papers have been turned in. Many different systems are possible. For example, you might have students put completed work in individual "mail boxes," then you can determine at a glance whose boxes are filled and whose are lacking assigned papers. Or you might have students put completed papers on a certain corner of their desks so that they will be easy to spot and check as you move around the room. This procedure is especially appropriate when you do not intend to collect the papers. A third procedure is to have students turn in their work to different baskets for each subject. You must find time to check each basket frequently and record each completed assignment in your grade book.

You should also give some attention to how you are going to collect work. When all students will be turning in materials at the same time, the most efficient procedure is to have the work passed in a given direction with no talking until you have them all in your hands. Materials such as workbooks that are inconvenient or bulky to pass might be collected by designated helpers and stacked in a particular spot. Papers or assignments that are turned in by students at varying times can be placed in appropriately labeled baskets, trays, or plastic containers. Avoid locating these drop-off spots in congested areas or where they might be distracting to nearby students. Be sure that students know the correct procedure you expect them to use. Following it consistently saves time and prevents confusion.

Maintaining Records of Student Work

An important part of your monitoring system is your record of student work completion. Generally these records will be a part of your grade book. You should organize the grade book so that you have a place for recording absent students each day, for example, by putting an a in the corner of the appropriate space. When setting up your grade book you can set aside several lines per student and record grades and scores for each subject on a separate line, or you can use a different page for each major subject. If you record grades for different subjects on the same line, you'll need a code such as different color pen or pencil to distinguish them. Or you can write in subject headings at the top of the page and separate them by heavy red vertical lines. If you have students from another teacher's class for instruction in a subject, be sure to leave space for those additional students on a page for that subject in your grade book. It will be your responsibility to supply the other teacher with report card evaluations, and it will be helpful to have all of the information in one place. Check with some experienced teachers at your grade level for suggestions on organizing your grade book.

You should record grades or other evaluations (E, S+, S, U) for major assignments and test results in your grade book. Whether to record an evaluation of other classwork such as worksheets or workbook pages is discretionary. This is not as common in the primary grades as in the intermediate grades, where more emphasis is placed on grading and a more complete record of daily work in major subjects is useful.

FEEDBACK TO STUDENTS

Good monitoring procedures provide the basis for feedback to students. Frequent and regular feedback is more desirable than sporadic appraisal because it reduces the amount of time students spend making errors if their performance is incorrect. Appropriate times for feedback will occur as you monitor work in progress and after it is completed. Try to give students immediate and specific feedback: Tell them what they need to do to correct errors, then check their corrections.

Feedback about completed work cannot occur until after the assignment has been checked. This should be done within a day of its completion so that the children will benefit from the feedback and you will be able to keep track of their progress. If you find yourself bogged down with work to check, have your students help you. At most grade levels students can exchange papers or check their own work (occasionally). Use student checkers only for work that they are capable of checking accurately, such as arithmetic worksheets or spelling quizzes. Displaying correct answers on the overhead projector can make checking work in class proceed smoothly and accurately. Generally the older the students, the more capable they are of accurate checking. Primary students cannot be expected to check anything but the simplest work. In the primary grades particularly, children's assignments are often short and easy to check quickly. Rather than collecting the work and checking it later, you can check each child's work as it is completed. Either have the student bring the work to you for checking or go around to each student (have them place the completed work in a corner of their desk so that it is easy to see). This practice gives prompt feedback to the students, cuts down considerably on the amount of paper shuffling you must do, and allows you to have students quickly correct their errors after receiving the feedback.

Pay careful attention at the beginning of the year to the completion of assignments. The first time a child fails to turn in an assignment without an apparent reason, talk with him or her about it. If the child

Reprinted by permission of King Feature Syndicate.

needs help, provide it, but require the child to do the work. If the child neglects two assignments consecutively or begins a pattern of skipping occasional assignments, call the parent(s) or send a note home. Be friendly, be encouraging, but insist that the work be done. Don't wait until the grading period is over to note problems with assignment completion or assume that the report card grade will communicate this information effectively. The parent or parents can be the teacher's strongest ally in assuring that the child takes school work seriously. And you should not hesitate to contact parents. Most parents will appreciate your concern and provide you with support from home.

Another procedure for communicating with parents is to have students take checked assignments home regularly. Be sure this includes good work and not just poor work. You can occasionally have parents sign and return the work as a way of rewarding and motivating students to "keep up the good work." Use a large envelope or a folder with two ends taped to convey the materials home rather than leave them loose. This envelope or folder also is a convenient receptacle for other important documents the child must transport home for signing or for the parents' information. Be sure the child's name is on the folder or envelope.

Another means of giving the children feedback is to display good work. Note that you should not make standards for "good" so stringent that some children can never meet them. Effort may be a more appropriate criterion in some cases.

Finally, teach students how to keep a record of their work. Older children can keep a sheet with test scores or assignment grades. Steps on a ladder or circles on a caterpillar to color in for each completed assignment or some other similar visual device can be a good motivator for some students.

SUGGESTED ACTIVITIES

1. The case studies at the end of the chapter illustrate effective accountability procedures. Decide which ones you can incorporate into your classroom.

2. Use Checklist 3 to organize your planning as you develop an accountability system.

CHECKLIST 3   Accountability Procedures

Area	Notes
I. Communicating Assignments and Work Requirements A. Where and how will you post assignments? B. What will be your standards for form and neatness? —Pencil, color of pen —Type of paper —Erasures —Due dates —Heading C. How will absent students know what assignments to make up? D. What will be the consequences of late or incomplete work?	
II. Monitoring Progress on and Completion of Assignments A. What procedures will you use to monitor work in progress? B. When and how will you monitor projects or longer assignments? C. How will you determine whether students are completing assignments? D. How will you collect completed assignments? E. What records of student work will you retain?	
III. Feedback A. What are your school's grading policies and procedures? B. What kinds of feedback will you provide, and when? C. What will you do when a student stops doing assignments? D. What procedure will you follow to send materials home to parents? E. Where will you display student work? F. What records, if any, of their own work will the students maintain?	

CASE STUDY 3–1:
PROCEDURES FOR MONITORING STUDENT PROGRESS

To help her students learn responsibility for their written work, Ms. Brown monitors student projects in class and promptly checks all papers. The first thing in the morning, she returns graded papers to students, who may then file correctly done work in their notebooks and correct all other papers before filing. Students with corrections to do are given help if necessary so they can complete them the same day.

When students work on written assignments in class, Ms. Brown circulates and systematically checks each student's progress. In addition, she has designated two class times for further progress checks. The first is in the fifteen minutes after returning from lunch, when Ms. Brown calls students up to her, one by one, to check their morning work while the rest of the class rests, takes turns using the bathroom, listens to a record, or reads library books. When assignments are incomplete, Ms. Brown discusses with the student how and when to finish. If the assignment can be checked quickly, Ms. Brown does so. For assignments too complex to grade quickly, she checks for completion and grades them later. Occasionally Ms. Brown uses this time to look over notebooks, checking for completeness and proper organization.

The second formal checking time is during the last few minutes of the school day. Ms. Brown maintains a list of assignments turned in during the day, and before students leave school she calls the names of those from whom she has not received certain papers saying, "I need a math (or spelling, handwriting, etc.) paper from these people." She posts the names of students who have completed the day's assignments on the chalkboard in a section labeled "Super People," and sometimes gives certificates of good performance to those who have worked especially well that day.

In addition to the two in-class checking periods, Ms. Brown uses spare moments to keep track of students as they are working. When time permits, she systematically walks around the room looking at each student's work, checking papers for correctness, and helping students with problems. She is careful to check frequently those students who are most likely to have difficulty with the work.

CASE STUDY 3–2:
KEEPING STUDENTS INVOLVED DURING A COMBINED
READING GROUP AND SEATWORK ACTIVITY

Ms. Avery designates a section of the chalkboard for listing seatwork assignments during reading group instruction. A typical assignment consists of three parts: a reading assignment, workbook pages, and comprehension questions and activities. At the beginning of the reading period, Ms. Avery presents directions for any seatwork assignment that is common to all groups. Then she assigns the group she will meet with first a brief "get ready" activity to complete and bring to the reading circle. She then gives instructions to the other groups, one at a time, for their seatwork. Each group is told when they can expect to be called and how much progress they should make. Before joining the first group, Ms. Avery quickly walks around the room to be sure each child has begun the seatwork assignment.

When she meets with each group (usually for fifteen to twenty minutes), she sits so she can see the entire class. She scans the class frequently and signals children when necessary to keep them on task. She does so by making eye contact or sometimes calling individual's names softly to prevent or stop inappropriate behavior. Because Ms. Avery does not want students coming to her for help while she is in the reading circle, she has assigned one helper for each reading group. In order to prevent excessive use of the helpers, Ms. Avery has taught the children to request assistance only for situations that prevent them from doing any work at all. If they can skip the problem or question and proceed with the work, they are to do so and wait for help from her.

As soon as she dismisses a reading group to begin a seatwork assignment, she circulates around the room checking on student progress, answering questions, helping students, and making sure that students in the most recent group have started their assignment promptly. Between groups, checks usually take no longer than five minutes, after which she is ready to call the next group.

If her work with one reading group lasts more than twenty minutes, Ms. Avery plans a short task for them to do independently at some point so she can leave the group to circulate among the students doing seatwork. She reminds students of how much time they have left and encourages those who are lagging behind.

After meeting with all the reading groups, Ms. Avery tells students how much more time they have to complete their seatwork activities. During those minutes, Ms. Avery again circulates, helping and prompting students who are still working and checking the work of students who have finished. By the end of the reading instruction period she has checked everyone's work. If students have not completed one or more of the seatwork assignments, Ms. Avery notes this and talks with them about when they can finish their work during the day.

CASE STUDY 3–3:
MATH ACCOUNTABILITY PROCEDURES
IN AN INTERMEDIATE GRADE

In Mr. Wilson's fifth-grade class, math always follows the morning break. At the end of the break, Mr. Wilson displays four or five math review problems on the overhead projector screen and then rings a bell to signal the end of the break. At this point students work the warm-up problems at their seats. Mr. Wilson sets a timer for five minutes and spends the time returning graded papers to students or taking care of other administrative matters. When math instruction begins, the warm-up problems are checked along with the regular assignment.

Mr. Wilson stresses the importance of being organized, and he has students keep a math folder with sections. The first section includes an assignment sheet on which students copy daily assignments. The second page in that section includes several reminders for math, such as, "Always use pencil. Copy the whole problem unless told otherwise." Other sections of the notebook include warm-ups, class and homework assignments, and tests.

When checking work in class, he has students exchange papers in a designated manner and sign their name on the paper they check. Mr. Wilson usually reads the answers and has students place an X next to incorrectly done problems. After checking they write the number of correct answers at the top of the page and return the papers to the owners for a discussion of any problems that have caused confusion. He then collects papers to check himself.

Mr. Wilson takes special care during the math lesson to present new material slowly and clearly, to check students' understanding of the processes involved, and to allow ample time for classroom practice and questions. When students begin working on the classwork assignment, he walks around the room, systematically looking at each student's paper. He helps those who request it, and only after the first ten minutes or so of student seatwork does he sit down to look over the homework and warm-up papers or to record grades. Students who need help while Mr. Wilson is at his desk raise their hands and are called up one at a time. If several students need help Mr. Wilson usually circulates around the class again.

The grading system is easily understood by students. The warm-ups for one grading period total one hundred problems and the number of correct answers counts as one test grade. Classwork and homework grades make up 50 percent of the total math average and tests contribute the remaining 50 percent. In addition, Mr. Wilson provides bonus questions on tests, interesting problems, and math puzzles that students can complete for extra credit if they finish their work before the end of the math period.

CHAPTER FOUR
REWARDS AND PENALTIES

Elementary grade children need incentives to encourage them to work hard, to complete assignments, and to follow classroom rules and procedures. In addition, penalties are sometimes needed to deter certain kinds of misbehavior or to handle it when it occurs. Of course, it would be ideal if all children had such strong motivation for learning everything that you want to teach and if their behavior were so angelic that you merely had to explain the rules and procedures to assure compliance. However, in the real world children's interests vary widely, school work is not always intrinsically exciting, and thirty children confined in a classroom for six or seven hours at a time will test the limits of any set of rules and procedures.

Whether your students will consistently follow your classroom rules and do their work depends in part on the *consequences*—both positive and negative—of cooperating or not cooperating. In this chapter two major types of consequences, rewards and penalties, will be described. A reward is something desirable that students receive in return for accomplishment, effort, or other appropriate behavior. A penalty is something undesirable that students must receive or do because their behavior was inappropriate. In this chapter we will be concerned only with the rewards and penalties that you can plan ahead of time and use as part of your overall system of classroom management. Other consequences that occur intrinsically (such as a feeling of satisfaction after completing a task) or that result from the reaction of one student to another are not controlled by the teacher and will not be discussed here.

Some general guidelines should be followed while planning rewards and penalties. You should first determine whether any local policies might affect your choice of consequences. For example, your school system may prohibit the use of particular rewards or penalties, and the school budget may not be able to afford the transportation costs for a field trip you wish to offer as a reward. Likewise, extensive busing or participation in after-school programs may conflict with the use of after-school detention as a penalty.

Your rewards and penalties should also be planned to suit the behaviors they are intended to encourage or deter. Rewards too easily earned or too difficult to achieve lose their motivational effect. Penalties that are harsh or too frequently used place the teacher in opposition to the students and invite criticism from parents. You should also be concerned about the use of reward or penalty systems that require you to use much class time for record keeping or other administration. Avoid using complex systems that distract you and your students from a focus on learning.

Finally, you should have some variety in your rewards. You can't count on a single type of reward to remain as a strong motivator for nine months. Use the ideas presented in this chapter, borrow some from other teachers or sources, and use your own experience to develop alternate strategies to use at different times of the year.

REWARDS

Many different types of rewards, including symbols, recognition, activities, and materials, can be used with elementary students. Each of these types is described below with examples.

Symbols. Elementary teachers use a variety of symbols to communicate a positive evaluation of student work. Examples include letter grades and numerical scores, happy faces, checks and check plusses, and stars and stickers with an appealing design. At all elementary grade levels, the teacher's positive evaluation and written comments are a source of satisfaction for students. For younger children, especially, this reward should be provided as soon as possible after they complete a task and on a daily basis. Assignments in the early grades

can usually be checked quickly, so there is no reason to delay feedback. One effective procedure for checking seatwork assignments such as worksheets, writing, or math is to have the children place them on a corner of their desks when finished. As you circulate through the room you can check completed assignments, write an E, put a star, check, or other symbol on the paper, and praise good effort, correctly done work, or neatness.

In the upper grades, where assignments are more complex or lengthy, you are more likely to collect assigned work in order to check it and record the grades in your grade book. Acquire a box of stars or other stickers, or buy hand stamps with a happy face or other symbols to supplement your numerical or letter grades. Be liberal in your use of these. Reward improvement and good effort so that all students have access to these incentives. Obviously, you should not reward poor performance, but do give feedback and encouragement so the student can improve.

In addition to their use for daily feedback, symbols are also used on report cards. Elementary grade children, even first graders, place a very positive value on high grades (or "lots of E's"), and it is not uncommon to hear young children comparing report card grades. However, most first or second graders are not likely to have a very clear conception of a specific relationship between daily work and long-term grades. Consequently, report card grades are not particularly useful incentives for encouraging young children to complete daily work. In the upper-elementary grades, however, students are better able to understand a connection between their work on daily assignments and the grades they receive in particular subjects. Therefore, it is a good idea to explain your grading policies to these children so that they will understand that the value you place on good effort and performance on daily work will translate into a report card grade. However, do not expect report card grades to be the major source of motivation for most students; plan to rely more on the daily use of symbols, positive feedback to students, and other rewards discussed below.

Recognition.   Recognition rewards involve some means of giving attention to the students. Examples are displaying student work; awarding a certificate for achievement, for impovement, or for good behavior; and verbally citing student accomplishments. Recognition rewards may be given on a weekly or monthly basis using some system such as "Super Stars of the Week," a class honor roll, or "Good Worker's Award." Be sure to explain the basis for awards—for example, good attendance, achievement, improvement, hard work, good conduct, or citizenship. The more *specific* you can be when describing the desired behavior, the more likely you will be to obtain it.

Some teachers encourage competition among student work teams or other groups. These competitions may be very simple and short (for example, in a first-grade class the teacher might say, "Let's see which table is ready first!"); at higher grade levels competitions may run for a week, a month, or a grading term and may be based on behavior or some specific academic task. If competition among groups is encouraged, this fact should be kept in mind when the teacher forms the groups. Group composition should be balanced so that all groups have an equal chance to succeed.

Activities.   Permitting or arranging for students to do something special or enjoyable constitutes giving an activity reward. Examples are privileges like free-reading time, game time, visits to the school library, or appointment as a room monitor, game leader or special helper. A more elaborate activity reward is the field trip or party. Because school policy may affect your use of the latter activities, you should clear any such activity with the appropriate administrator before announcing it to your class. You should of course be certain to describe clearly what students need to do to receive such privileges.

Material incentives.   Material incentives are objects of value to students. Examples include food, a pencil or eraser, discarded classroom materials, games, toys, or books. You will have to consider your own financial circumstances as well as school policy before deciding to use such rewards.

A procedure combining several types of rewards is the use of an honor roll system (an all-star list, super stars, gold record club) or competition among groups or teams in conjunction with other incentives. Badges, stickers with appealing designs, food treats, activity privileges, or a party can be used as rewards along with the recognition of being an award winner. It is best to spread the honors around and include a good portion of the class. Do not give awards only for outstanding achievement; have awards for improvement, excellent effort, good conduct, and so on.

When using a class party or field trip as an activity reward, you will need to be particularly careful. If only half the class can meet the criteria you establish for receiving this award, you will also have to figure out what to do with a large number of unhappy students during the party or field trip. For such a reward, it would be better to establish criteria that all students could meet (such as good citizenship). In this way you can encourage a class norm for good behavior that is attainable by everyone, and you will not risk the problems that can arise if students must compete for scarce rewards.

A major consideration in the use of rewards is their feasibility. Some rewards require a great deal of planning, record keeping, or other preparation. For example a field trip, party, or major group activity needs careful planning. If some (presumably a very few) students will be denied the activity, then arrangements must be made for their supervision during it. In addition, transportation may need to be arranged, other adults may be needed for supervision, and some expense may be incurred. Other rewards require very little preparation or effort. Examples are giving positive verbal feedback, placing a symbol or some other positive comment on an assignment sheet, and awarding simple privileges such as leading the line to lunch, passing out materials, taking up papers, and being a room monitor.

Between the two extremes of much effort and very little effort are a large number of rewards that require a modest amount of the teacher's time or effort. These include things such as awarding free time for reading, play, or games; sending home a positive note to parents; awarding prizes such as a pencil with the school name on it; allowing extra time in the library or for some other activity; and establishing an honor roll or "Super Star" list. Don't try too much too soon in the way of reward systems. Systems that require extensive record keeping or constant attention or complex arrangements will be a substantial drain on your time. Start with simple procedures and add to them if you can. The case studies at the end of the chapter illustrate a number of possibilities.

PENALTIES

The rewards described in the previous section will help motivate appropriate behavior, but they will not be sufficient to prevent all disruption or other inappropriate behaviors. Penalties are necessary to deter violations of rules and procedures. It should be noted that penalties are not needed or even desirable for all rule and procedure violations. Many such violations can be handled by simple, direct teacher actions; such strategies will be described in detail in Chapter Six. However, you need to have penalties available in case serious infractions occur. Planning ahead for penalties will not only serve as a deterrent, but will also give you a standard, consistent response to particular classes of misbehaviors.

Students should be informed of what your penalties are and how they will be used. This can be done when you discuss your rules and procedures. Of course, you should avoid a threatening or negative tone. The best approach is to describe major penalties in a matter-of-fact manner and tie each to the behavior it is intended to deter. You do not necessarily have to describe all school-prescribed consequences (such as in-school suspension for fighting) or consequences for behaviors that are rare or for which the consequence is obvious. Such events can be handled if and when they occur, as long as you know what the penalties are.

The types of inappropriate behavior for which teachers often assess penalties include incomplete, missing, or poorly done assignments; abusive name calling or other aggression; and repeated violations of classroom rules or procedures. Commonly used penalties are described below. More extensive treatment of how they can be used with particular types of misbehavior is presented in Chapter Six in the section dealing with special problems. We do not recommend that you try to adopt all of these penalties for use in your classroom. Instead, select a subset that will be easy to administer and that you are comfortable with using.

Reduction in score or grade.   At the upper elementary grades this is the most common type of penalty for late, incomplete, or missing assignments and poorly done work. When you determine your grading criteria, decide on appropriate penalties. Teachers often use the following: A score of zero or a grade of F for missing assignments (without a valid excuse) and a reduction in grade for incomplete work. Some teachers accept unexcused late work for certain assignments but reduce the grade; other teachers refuse to accept it and require that students turn in whatever they have done when it is due and accept the consequences if it is incomplete. At all grade levels symbols can be used to communicate dissatisfaction with student work. The use of a "check minus" or a U is common when grades or numerical scores are not assigned. Too heavy a dose of these can dampen the most enthusiastic student's spirits, so go easy on them. It's probably best to reserve these for slipshod, lackadaisical effort. Rely primarily on corrective feedback and encouragement to help struggling students.

Loss of privileges.   This is one of the more effective penalties because in most cases the penalty can be assessed to fit the "crime." For example, if talking becomes excessive during seatwork, the class or the student can lose the privilege of talking (assuming you allowed it in the first place). Students who abuse equipment can be denied access to it for a period of time. A student who bothers others must sit alone. In other words, if a student abuses a privilege, it is withdrawn. If you are using a reward system such as a "Super Stars of the Week" or class honor roll, then violations of particular rules may result in losing one's place on the list and whatever other rewards are associated with it.

Fines. This does not refer to money, but rather to "payment" in the form of (usually) repetitious work. For example, a student might be required to copy a standard paragraph, sentences, spelling words, or mathematics tables. This type of penalty is generally used for repeated violations of some classroom rule or procedure (disruptive talk, wandering) rather than for serious violations such as aggression toward another student.

Detention after school. This penalty requires that students stay with you in your classroom or else go to a designated room monitored by some other adult. Detention is frequently assessed for violations of some major school or classroom rule or for chronic misbehavior. Its advantages include the opportunity for a private conference with the student to try to work out a long-range solution to the problem.

Check or demerit systems. These are used in conjunction with other penalties. A student who violates an important rule receives a check or demerit. The teacher either records this on a chalkboard, in the grade book, or on another record sheet. Checks or demerits are usually used on a daily basis. The first demerit can serve as a warning; the second and any other demerit received that day causes a penalty (such as a fine) to be assessed. The slate is then wiped clean each day.

Referral to the principal. This penalty is best reserved for serious infractions. In addition the violation of certain school rules will call for this penalty as a school policy.

Restitution. This penalty requires the student to repair damage or to pay money for replacement of lost or damaged property.

Confiscation. This is the loss of possession of objects forbidden on school property or in the classroom. Depending on the object, the student may have it back at the end of the day, may be required to retrieve it from the school office, or may permanently lose possession of it.

"Back again, Master Biggs?"

Determining Appropriate Penalties

In some cases the choice of penalties will be governed by school policy. You can determine which of these penalties to use in your classes by examining your rules and procedures and becoming familiar with any schoolwide system in use. The following guidelines are offered.

1. For missing or incomplete work, use immediate feedback, reductions in score or grade, and/or keep the student after school to complete the work. When chronic missing work occurs, contact the student's parents, talk with the student, and try to get at the source of the problem.

2. Use a fine or demerit system and/or the loss of privileges to handle repeated violations of rules and procedures, particularly willful refusal to comply with reasonable requests. Such behaviors include continual talking that interferes with whole-class instruction and disruptive out-of-seat behavior. You will not need penalties to handle occasional occurrences of these types of inappropriate behaviors (see Chapter Six); however, students who persist in such behavior need a penalty for a deterrent. Give them one warning, and if the behavior persists, assess a penalty.

3. If you have a student who frequently receives penalties, try to set a more positive tone. Help the student formulate a plan to stop the inappropriate behavior and be sure he or she understands what is and is not acceptable to you.

4. Limit the use of penalties such as fines or demerits to easily observable behaviors that represent major infractions of rules and procedures. The reason for this limitation is that penalty systems work only when they are used consistently. In order to do so, you must be able to detect the misbehavior when it occurs. If you cannot, then you will find yourself constantly trying to catch

students who misbehave. To illustrate, don't try to fine each student who whispers during seatwork. You can handle such events in simpler ways, and you certainly don't want to spend all your time checking for whispering behavior. However, you can use a penalty or "time out" if the student does not stop when you request it. Examples of penalties are provided in the case studies at the end of the chapter.

5. Keep your classroom atmosphere positive and supportive. Penalties should serve mainly as deterrents and should be used sparingly. Try to rely on rewards and personal encouragement to maintain good behavior.

SUGGESTED ACTIVITIES

1. Read the case studies at the end of this chapter and consider how you might adapt these examples of reward and penalty system to your own classroom.

2. Find out about school policies that affect your use of rewards and penalties. Also, note any schoolwide system that you will need to incorporate into your own classroom procedures.

3. Review Checklists 2 and 3 and identify the rewards and penalties you intend to use with your major conduct and accountability procedures. By planning ahead you will be better able to explain these consequences and to be consistent in their use.

CASE STUDY 4–1: THREE DIFFERENT REWARD
AND PENALTY SYSTEMS

Ms. Hardy used a consequence system called "Shoot for the Moon" to give feedback to second-grade students for behavioral and academic performance. She decorated a large bulletin board with blue paper, a large round moon, a few clouds, and a title, "Shoot for the Moon". Each child's name was written on a small, construction paper spaceship. The spaceships were lined up at the bottom of the bulletin board at the start. At the beginning of the year Ms. Hardy discussed with her class the kinds of behaviors that would result in the movement of each spaceship closer to the moon. Daily completion of assignments and good behavior in the classroom, at lunch, and on the playground would result in the spaceship moving two inches closer to the moon. For bad behavior (such as misbehavior in the lunchroom or during instruction, not working in class, or not turning in an assignment) a student's spaceship would be moved one inch away from the moon. When students reached the moon, they were rewarded by being able to keep their spaceships decorated with a star. The teacher then started another spaceship for them at the bottom of the board. Sometimes students were required to reach the moon by a certain deadline in order to get a special reward such as a privilege or a popcorn party. Ms. Hardy was consistent in rewarding appropriate behavior each day and penalizing inappropriate behaviors, and she also occasionally rewarded individual students for being especially quiet or helpful or for improving their work or grades. This worked well with students who had particular behavior or academic problems.

Ms. Harmony's class functioned smoothly and productively without many obvious rewards and penalties. Although she only occasionally rewarded individuals or groups with public compliments, Ms. Harmony maintained a high level of student involvement through interesting, well-paced lessons and assignments with a high level of student success, and by promptly returning assignments and giving students feedback regarding their work. She dealt with inappropriate behavior by brief verbal correction of students or short private conferences with individuals inside the classroom. Often she would simply mention what the student should be doing if all the rest of his or her work was finished. Penalties she used were keeping a student in during recess or putting a student's desk in the hall outside the door. Ms. Harmony made extensive use of telephone contacts with parents to inform them of their children's progress and particularly to identify when a student was not completing assignments satisfactorily. She did this frequently during the first few months of the school year, with long-lasting results.

Mr. Young used a variety of strategies, some simple and some elaborate, for encouraging appropriate behavior in his third-grade class. Throughout the year he used a system in which the class as a whole earned blue chips for good behavior and red chips for poor behavior. When a monthly goal for the number of blue chips was reached, the class was rewarded with a treat or special privilege. Goals and rewards escalated during the course of the year, beginning with a class party at the end of the first month and culminating in a field trip to a state fair. During each day blue chips were dropped into a container for various appropriate behaviors—two for good behavior during the time a visitor was in the room, ten for each satisfactory cleanup, one for each student who at the end of the day had completed his or her contract work, and so on. Red chips were dropped into the container for excessive noise, throwing trash on the floor, bad behavior on the way to lunch, or other transgressions. Shaking the can that contained the chips was often used to signal that there was too much talking or misbehaving and that failure to get quiet would result in another red chip. At the end of the day red chips were counted and an equal number of blue chips were deducted from the blue chip collection.

In addition to the chip system, Mr. Young complimented good workers aloud, sometimes let best-behaved or best-prepared students line up first, put names of cooperative students on the board under a "Superpeople" title, and awarded happy faces to students who did all of their work that day. For deterrents, he made an unruly student work at a special desk near his, held conferences, dismissed students one or two minutes late, asked transgressors to state the rule or proper procedure, or stopped an enjoyable activity until individuals or the class corrected their behavior.

CHAPTER FIVE
GETTING OFF
TO A GOOD START

The beginning of school is an important time for classroom management because your students will learn behavior, attitudes, and work habits that will affect them the rest of the year. Of course, it is better if they start the year behaving appropriately rather than practicing sloppy work habits and misbehavior.

Your major goal for the beginning of the year is to obtain student cooperation in two key areas: following your rules and procedures and successfully completing all work assignments. Attaining this goal will make it possible for you to create a good environment for learning during the rest of the year.

A concern for establishing appropriate behavior does not imply a lack of concern for student feelings and attitudes. Instead, the intent is to create a classroom climate that helps children feel secure and that prevents problems from occurring. In addition, some of the suggestions in this chapter will focus directly on cognitive goals, while others will incorporate student concerns and other affective considerations.

The major topics in this chapter are teaching your rules and procedures to the students, deciding on the classroom activities you will use during the first week of school, arranging these activities into workable lesson plans, and identifying needed materials. Finally, some special problems are discussed. A checklist is available to help organize your planning, and two case studies of the beginning of the year will give you many ideas about how to begin.

TEACHING RULES AND PROCEDURES

One of the surest ways to communicate your expectations for student behavior is through a planned system of classroom rules and procedures. How best to teach this system to your students is an important consideration. The term *teach* is used purposely; you will not communicate your expectations adequately if you only *tell* students about rules and procedures.

Three aspects of the teaching process are important:

Describing and demonstrating the desired behavior.   Use words and actions to convey what behavior is acceptable or desirable. Be as specific as possible. For example, do not simply tell the children you expect them to be good while you are out of the room; tell them what "be good" means—stay in seats, no talking, keep working. You should demonstrate desired behavior whenever possible. For example, if you are going to allow "quiet talking" or "classroom voices" during seatwork, then you should provide demonstrations of what this means. If the procedure is complex, then present it in a step-by-step manner. For example, lining up requires that students know when to line up (e.g., the teacher gives permission by tables or rows), where and how to go (e.g., push chairs under tables and then walk without talking), expected behavior in line (e.g., hands off others, no talking in halls, walk—don't run). You do not need to do all the demonstrating; many students enjoy the privilege of showing the class the correct procedure.

Rehearsal.   This means practicing the behaviors. Rehearsal serves two purposes: It helps children learn the appropriate behavior, and it provides you with an opportunity to determine whether the children understand and can correctly follow a procedure. Complex procedures may have to be rehearsed several times. This aspect of teaching procedures is especially helpful for primary-grade children; however, the older elementary school child can benefit from rehearsal whenever the procedures are complex or have not previously been encountered.

Feedback.   After you have asked students to follow a procedure for the first time, be sure to tell them if they did it properly and praise them if they did. If improvement is needed be sure to tell them that too. Be discriminating in your feedback—for example, "I liked how quickly you put your materials away, but I did not like the talking by the students at Table Two." If many students do not follow a procedure correctly, then you should repeat one or more of the above steps. If only a few students are off track, then you might have some other students show them what to do. You can also ask students who are not following your procedure to describe what they are supposed to do, so that you can determine whether they understand your directions. Finally, the fact that students follow the procedure correctly once does not mean that they will do so consistently. You should watch them carefully and be prepared to give reminders and feedback as appropriate.

Two examples that illustrate how to teach procedures are presented below. The first example shows the teacher instructing students on the use of the correct heading on their papers. This procedure was taught to students on the first day of school in a fourth-grade class as part of an assignment to write a brief account of their summer.

> Mr. Samuels has written a sample heading for students' papers on the front chalkboard. He points to it, explaining to students that he wants this heading to be on every assignment they do. He points to the upper right-hand corner of the sample page and explains that students should write the heading there. Mr. Samuels then tells students they should write both their first and last names on the first line. He points to the line below where he has written "Writing" and explains that this line is for the subject of the assignment and will change when students do an assignment in another subject. Students are then instructed to put the date with the month spelled out under the subject name. The teacher points out the room calendar and suggests that students refer to it when they need to know the date. Mr. Samuels then asks the class if there are any questions about the heading. When no questions are forthcoming, Mr. Samuels tells the students to take out a sheet of paper and pencil and to put the correct heading for a writing lesson on their paper. He then circulates around the room, checking to make sure that every student is using the proper heading.

Note that Mr. Samuels demonstrated the correct form by having an example on the chalkboard; he described each aspect carefully and gave students an immediate opportunity to practice the heading and to receive corrective feedback.

The next example shows how a complex transition procedure was taught to a second-grade class. The teacher in this example teaches students to respond to a signal, put away their materials, and move to a rug area.

> Ms. Stevens explains to her students that she expects them to move quickly and quietly from one activity to another so that they will have time to do all the things that are planned. She shows them the kitchen timer and makes it ring. She tells the students that this will be a very important signal. When they hear this bell, the students should put away the materials they are using and move to the next activity as quickly as possible. "After reading I will ring the bell and then you are to put your reading materials in your desk as quickly as possible. You should then get up from your desk and walk carefully and quietly to the rug so that we can begin our Spanish lesson. Are there any questions?" A student asks if she will always ring the bell for Spanish and Ms. Stevens says she will.
>
> Ms. Stevens then tells the class that she would like them to practice. "You have paper and pencil on your desk that you have been using to write a story. I will give you time to finish the story later in the day. Right now, when I ring the bell you should put your materials in your desk and come quickly and quietly to the rug." At this point Ms. Stevens rings the bell. Students immediately begin putting away their materials and moving toward the rug. However, several students line up to get drinks of water and one goes to the bathroom. When everyone is on the rug in a circle around Ms. Stevens, she refers to the clock on the wall and says, "It took us three minutes to put the materials away and get to the rug. You are second graders now, and I think you can move faster than that. I think you should be seated on the rug in a circle in one minute. Also, it was not time to get a drink of water or to use the bathroom unless it was an emergency. Do you all understand?" The students all nod solemnly.
>
> Ms. Stevens then tells students to return to their desks, get out their paper and pencils, and get set to practice again. The students go quickly back to their desks, and take out their materials. Ms. Stevens then rings the bell again, and students go through the routine, this time more quickly. After all the students are settled Ms. Stevens smiles and thanks the students, "You've done a super job. It only took you one minute to get to the rug. I'm really proud of you."

In the above example Ms. Stevens demonstrated the signal, described the desired behavior, and gave a rationale for it. The students were allowed to practice the process twice, and feedback was given to them each time.

PLANNING FOR A GOOD BEGINNING

You have already done a major portion of the planning for the beginning of the year if you have followed the guidelines in the first four chapters. Your room should be arranged, and you will have decided on your rules, procedures, rewards, and penalties. You now need to plan activities for the first several days of school.

Important Considerations

For the first days of school you should plan activities that will allow all your students to be successful. Such activities will make students feel more secure and confident and encourage their continued good effort. Initial lesson and seatwork assignments should be easy and require only simple directions. In this way the children will quickly learn lesson routines and encounter little difficulty in completing assignments.

Plan activities with a whole-class focus. For the first few days you should limit the lessons to those that can be presented and explained to all the students at the same time. Do not try to group students for instruction for at least several days, and if you can, avoid individual testing or any activities or seatwork assignments that require you to work with individual students for long periods of time. Don't overload yourself or your students with unnecessarily complicated activities. Your students will already be learning many new procedures during the first few days of school. In addition, you will need to be free to watch students very carefully during the first few days in order to detect problems and take appropriate action. If you are involved with a small group or with an individual, you may not see important behaviors and events.

Plan your activities to take into account the children's perspectives, concerns, and needs for information about the new and unfamiliar situation that your classroom presents. A variety of activities, including some with physical movement and music, and provision for occasional short breaks will provide the changes of pace that help maintain interest and alertness throughout the day. In addition, you should stimulate the children's interest in the curriculum and associated activities. If you are excited about the wonderful things they will be learning this year, your students are more likely to feel that enthusiasm themselves. Foreshadow some of the interesting units in science and social studies, or tell them about some of the skills that they will develop in your class.

Some Typical Activities

Activities that you will use in the first school day and for several days thereafter are described below. They are not necessarily presented in the sequence you will use, nor will you use each one every day, so you should carefully examine the two case studies at the end of the chapter in order to see how different teachers put the pieces together.

Greeting the students. Prepare student name tags ahead of time. Have extra materials on hand for unexpected students. Decide how name tags will be fastened. If you use straight pins you may be inviting little dueling matches and surprise pricks and pokes. If you intend to use safety pins, be sure your students can fasten them or plan to do it for them. Other options are tape, commercial stick-on tags, or a length of yarn to allow the name tags to be worn like a necklace. Instead of using name tags, you might also tape a card onto the top of the student's desk and write the student's name on it.

When students enter the room greet them warmly, help them get their name tags on, and get them seated. If you have taped their names to a desk, then the matter of seating is settled. In some cases, however, the roster of students is not definite, and you may not want to bother setting up a seating chart before the students arrive. In this case let the students choose their desks. (Make a seating chart and/or label desks with name tags as soon as practicable, making any necessary adjustments later.) Don't allow the students to wander around the room or to get loud. If students straggle in and you cannot start class right away, provide a simple dittoed worksheet, a dot-to-dot drawing, or a picture to color, so that students will have something to do at their desks. As soon as most students are present, begin with the introduction.

Introductions. You will want to tell the students something about yourself; however, an extended autobiography is not necessary. A few personal notes and something about your interests would be appropriate. Have students introduce themselves—nothing more than a name is necessary, but some teachers like to use a little more introduction, having the children tell something about themselves. The introduction activity should not take too long, however, as there will be plenty of opportunity later to get acquainted.

Room description. You'll need to point out major areas of the room, particularly any areas that students will be using on the first day. As you do so, any procedures associated with room use that will be needed that day should be described to students. For example, show students where they may put their coats, lunches, or other items they bring from home; be sure they know where the pencil sharpener is and when they may use it, where frequently used supplies are stored, the location of the calendar, wastebasket, and clock, and so on.

Get-acquainted activities.   Teachers frequently include a get-acquainted activity as part of their first day plan. Such activities can help children feel that the teacher and other children know them better and care about them as individuals. Teachers often describe the goal of such an activity as helping students feel more comfortable with their classmates and more secure. The activities are also used to foster a greater sense of class cohesiveness. One of the examples of get-acquainted activities described below can be used early in the first day's plan of activities. It will provide a nice change of pace after the room description or after the initial discussion of rules and major procedures.

Ask students to introduce themselves and to name a favorite activity or hobby, or tell about something they did during the summer. Keep this activity moving briskly because student attention will wane during long introductions. A variation of this activity is to use reciprocal introductions. Have pairs of students learn each other's name and something about the other person (hobbies, interests). Then have each person introduce his or her partner.

Use a name game to help students remember names and to add interest to introductions. For example, have students make up an adjective to go with their own name (e.g., Happy Holly, Curious Carl) or have students think of a food they like (Milk-Shake Marty, Sauerkraut Sarah). Then as students introduce themselves have them name the other students who came before them (or perhaps the last five students) along with their adjectives or foods.

Make ditto copies of a line drawing of the school's mascot. Then have each child sign his or her copy and write some personal facts (names of brothers or sisters, pets; likes and dislikes; favorite activities, foods, and so forth) on the drawing. Post these on a bulletin board so students can read about each other.

Have students complete a brief questionnaire identifying interests, favorite subjects, family members, etc.

The activities decribed below can be used the first day or later in the week, after students are more acquainted with one another or after you have time to prepare for the activity.

Make a puzzle with student names. For example, leave out a few letters in each name for students to fill in. Or list first and last names in separate columns in scrambled order and let students match names; or students can identify names arranged in a "seek and find" puzzle.

Set aside a few minutes before the children leave, in order to review the day's activities and to discuss with the students what they learned, found difficult, liked best, and so forth. Say a few words about upcoming events and activities that the children will look forward to. Comment on good work and behavior to reinforce your expectations and to keep the tone positive.

Have students from last year's class—you'll need to plan this well ahead—write letters to students in this year's class, telling them what to expect, what was fun about the year, suggestions for study, and what they learned during the year. Share these letters with your students.

Have students bring a paper bag with three to five objects, such as books, pictures, or toys, that tell something about themselves. Let students use these props to introduce themselves on the second or third day of school. Split the activity into two segments if necessary to maintain attention and interest.

Make up a questionnaire in the form of a scavenger hunt; for example, "Name a student who has three brothers and who plays kick-ball." Let students work in groups to see how many of their classmates they can identify.

Presentation and discussion of rules, procedures, and consequences. Soon after the introductions, usually after the initial room description, you should conduct the first presentation of major rules and procedures. School rules should be covered along with your classroom rules. Major consequences associated with the rules should also be described at the same time. You should plan to review the rules later, perhaps on the second and third days, to confirm their importance and help students remember them. Posting the rules will also serve as a reminder to students. Important procedures should also be taught. Teach these procedures as they are needed, rather than all at once. For example, during this initial discussion you will probably want to teach procedures for using bathroom and pencil sharpener, moving about the room, obtaining help, asking questions, and talking. Later in the day, as they are needed, teach other important procedures such as procedures for major transitions (ending the day, leaving and entering the room at lunch time, etc.) as well as procedures associated with recess, cafeteria, or other out-of-room areas. Your opening routine (see Chapter Two) will probably be used on the second day of school, so you may wish to wait until then to go through it with the students. Procedures for special equipment can wait until you're ready to use a particular piece of equipment, and small group procedures should not be introduced until those activities are to begin. The idea is to provide students with the information they need to complete successfully the activities required of them in the first few days of school and to help them feel confident in their new classroom environment.

THE FAMILY CIRCUS®   **By Bil Keane**

"The hardest part about goin' back to school is learning how to whisper again."

The Family Circus, Reprinted Courtesy The Register and Tribune Syndicate, Inc.

On the second day of school you should review the rules and some of the major procedures students need to know. This reinforces your expectations for appropriate behavior and reminds students of rules and procedures they may have forgotten. When correcting students' behavior at the beginning of school, it is important to remind students of what rule was broken. In the primary grades particularly, you will need to observe students carefully for several weeks to be sure they are following procedures correctly and to give reminders, cues, and prompting to help them learn class routines.

Content activities.   Be sure to select activities that are uncomplicated and that can be presented to the whole class. Seatwork assignments should allow for differences in speed of completion; be sure to have some back-up activities for students who complete work early. Consult your teacher's manuals and curriculum guides and talk with experienced teachers to get ideas about appropriate beginning content activities for different subjects at your grade level.

Time fillers.   Periodically, you will need to fill in time between activities or before and after major transitions. For example, students may complete a seatwork assignment earlier then you anticipated, but there may not be enough time to begin another activity before the next scheduled event. Or there may be times when the students need a short break after an intensive lesson. Filling these times with constructive activity is better than trying to stretch out an already completed task or just letting students amuse themselves. Some ideas include having a good book to read to the children or some simple games that can be played in the classroom (such as Seven Up, Name Bingo, Hangman, Baseball Math, Spelling Bee). Keep on hand some dittos or other handouts with puzzles, riddles, or pictures to color. You can also lead the children in group exercises, sing songs, or listen to a good children's record. Ask other teachers for ideas and accumulate a file so that you will be ready with a filler whenever one is needed.

Administrative activities.   You will need to distribute textbooks to students. You may wish to issue one or two textbooks on the first day; some teachers wait a day or two before distributing textbooks and use handouts and dittos for assignments, especially if class enrollment is likely to change. When you do give out books, you need to record book numbers for each student, perhaps using a standard form. You should also determine school policies in this area. For example, some schools require that books issued to students be kept covered at all times. If so, you will need a supply of covers on hand and you will need to be prepared to teach the children how to cover the books. In lower grades, it might be better to do the job yourself or enlist the help of parents or an aide. Even in higher grades, some students will have forgotten how to cover books. Plan to show the whole class, and schedule plenty of time for this event.

Determine whether there are any materials that students must take home with them on the first day or later in the week (this might include information about the breakfast and lunch program, school policy on attendance, time of arrival and departure for children, etc.). A good idea is to prepare a letter to send home to parents explaining any essential information that is not already conveyed via school handouts. Sometimes teachers at one grade level get together and collaborate on the letter. If not, write one of your own and get it ready to go home with the children at the end of the first day. Its purpose is to establish a link with parents and to communicate important information to them. The letter should include information on:

> Materials or supplies their child will need
>
> Your conference times and how parents may contact you
>
> Information on breakfast and lunch programs if not already provided by the school
>
> Any special information you want them to know

A cheerful, friendly letter that is neat, legible, grammatically correct, and free of misspellings will create a good impression and communicate a professional image to the parents. It is easy to get extremely rushed at the beginning of the year and to let this letter be slipshod. Have a friend proofread the letter before you duplicate it to be sure it is clear and easy to read.

Special Problems

While it is not possible to predict every problem that could occur in the first few days of school, it is possible to identify several that occur commonly, occasionally, or rarely. If you are prepared for the commonly occurring problems and at least not surprised by the occasional or rare event, you will be able to cope.

1. Interruptions by office staff, parents, custodians, and others (common). If you can manage the interruption without leaving the room, do so. Ask the interrupter into your room and face your children as you talk with the person. If the interruption is likely to last more than a few seconds or if you must leave the room, give the children something to do before continuing the conference. Let the interrupter wait, not your class. Ask your students to continue working if they are already involved in an activity. If not, tell them that they can use the time to read a book that they have at their desk or to rest their heads on their desks.

2. Late arrivals on the first day (common). Greet late arrivals as warmly as you did the other students. Tell them you will talk to them about what they missed as soon as you can, but that for now they must wait in their seats. Show them where to sit. When you have the total class involved in some seatwork activity, meet with these children to explain anything they may have missed.

3. One or more children are assigned to your class after the first day (common). Try to arrange to meet with these students before school so that you can explain rules and procedures to them and handle necessary paper work. If you have already distributed books to the class, make sure these students also get texts. If you can't meet these students ahead of time, use the first available opportunity, while the rest of your class is occupied with seatwork. Appoint one or more responsible students to be "buddies" with the new student to help familiarize them with the classroom and school procedures and rules. The amount of assistance you can expect from these buddies will depend on their grade level. Be sure to monitor new students carefully to help them adjust to your class and to learn appropriate behavior.

4. The school or district office requires you to complete large amounts of paperwork during the first week of school (occasional). Do as little of this during class time as possible. Plan to spend extra time before and after school and arrange your personal schedule to accommodate it. This will pay off in reduced tension over the long run. If you must do clerical work during class time, do it during short periods of time when the children are engaged in seatwork activities. Monitor the class while you work.

5. Insufficient numbers of textbooks are available or vital equipment and materials are missing (occasional). Before school begins, you should check on the availability of textbooks and your equipment and find out your school's procedures for getting the needed materials into your room. When you discover shortages, report them to the proper person from the school office. If you must begin the year without enough texts, you may be able to have students share books or you might arrange to share a class set with another teacher. If you have no texts at all in some subject, you can probably find earlier editions of the text in the book storage room to tide you over. Depending on the subject, dittos or other teacher-prepared materials may be sufficient.

6. One of your students has a handicap that seriously interferes with his or her ability to understand you or to follow directions (occasional). Seat the child close to you and engage him or her in simple activities. Work individually with this student only after the rest of the class is busy. As soon as possible, talk to the child's resource teacher to determine what the child is capable of doing, then plan the child's educational program. If possible, talk to the child's teacher from the preceding year for suggestions. You will also find it helpful to set up a conference with the child's parents soon after the year has begun.

7. A child becomes very sick or is injured (rare). If the child has a known medical condition (such as epilepsy) and you have been previously informed of what to do, follow directions and stay calm. In other cases, phone the office or send a messenger requesting someone to come to get the child. Do not leave the child unattended.

8. Crying (occasional). Younger children especially may tend to cry for no apparent reason early in the school year. The crying will usually stop fairly quickly if you can distract the child and engage him or her in some activity. Sometimes it helps to assign a friend to accompany the child to get a drink of water, wash his or her face, and then come back to join the class. Be understanding but do not reinforce crying by giving the child excessive attention or sympathy. If the crying is not disruptive, the child can remain in his or her seat until the episode is over. If the crying is disruptive, take the child out of the room or have someone from the office come to get him or her.

9. Wetting (occasional).   While accidental wetting is more common with younger children, it sometimes occurs even in the upper grades, especially during the first few days of school. This kind of accident is extremely embarrassing to the child, and the teacher should make every effort not to add to the child's discomfort. Have some paper towels on hand to facilitate the cleanup and handle the matter as privately as possible. You should arrange to call home or have an office worker phone to bring a change of clothes to school. Later, talk privately with the child to determine why he or she did not go to the restroom in time. With some younger children, you may need to contact the parents and keep a change of clothes at school as a precaution. In general with younger children, the teacher needs to schedule regular bathroom breaks and even remind some children to use the bathroom regularly.

Checklist 4, which follows the chapter activities, covers areas discussed in this chapter and items that will help to prepare for the beginning of school.

SUGGESTED ACTIVITIES

1. Read the case studies at the end of the chapter and use these to help prepare your lesson plans for the beginning of school.

2. Use Checklist 4 to organize your planning activities.

3. Talk with some teachers who have had several years of experience at the grade level you will be teaching. Ask them what activities they use during the first few days and how they sequence them. Teachers are often willing to share handouts and ideas. You might also ask someone to look over your lesson plan for the first day and give you suggestions.

CHECKLIST 4   Preparation for the Beginning of School

Item	Check When Ready	Notes
1. Are your room and materials ready (see Chapter One)?		
2. Have you decided on your class procedures, rules, and associated consequences (see Chapters Two, Three, and Four)?		
3. Are you familiar with the parts of the school that you and your students may use (cafeteria, office and office phone, halls, bathroom facilities, resource room, etc.) and any procedures associated with their use?		
4. Do you have a complete class roster?		
5. Do you have file information on your students, including information on reading and math achievement levels from previous teachers, test results, and any other information?		
6. Do you know if any of your students have handicapping conditions that should be accommodated in your room arrangement or in your instruction?		
7. Do you have adequate numbers of textbooks, desks, and class materials?		
8. Do you have teacher's editions of your textbooks?		
9. Do you know the procedure for the arrival and departure of students on the first day? For every day after that?		
10. Are the children's name tags ready? Do you have some blank ones for unexpected children?		
11. Do you have your first day's plan of activities ready?		
12. Does your daily schedule accommodate special classes (e.g., P.E., music) or "pull-out" programs (e.g., Chapter I reading, resource room students, special programs for the gifted)?		
13. Do you have time-filler activities prepared?		
14. Do you have a letter ready to send home to parents with information on what materials the children will need to bring to school?		
15. Do you know when and how you can obtain assistance from school staff members (e.g., the resource teacher, school nurse, librarian, office personnel, counselor)?		

CASE STUDY 5-1: BEGINNING THE SCHOOL YEAR IN AN INTERMEDIATE GRADE

The First Day

Time	Description	Activity
8:00–8:04	Ms. Beech greets students individually as they enter the room, and she gives each a stick-on name tag. "Your desk is the one with your name on the card taped on it," she tells them, "and you may work on the puzzle page that is in your desk or you may wait quietly until I begin class." After the school bell rings, Ms. Beech greets a few late-comers and chats briefly with two parents while the children work on the puzzles. Then she addresses the class, telling them to put the puzzle page in their desks for now and that they will be able to work on it later. She waits while students put the puzzle sheet away.	Greeting students
8:04–8:09	Ms. Beech then introduces herself and talks briefly about where she taught last year. She tells the class about the good things she has heard about them from their former teachers. She says that she has high expectations for this class. Then she asks each student to stand and say his or her name and tell where he or she went to school last year. Ms. Beech checks the roll at the same time.	Introductions
8:09–8:16	Ms. Beech distributes letters that were written by her students from the previous year's class. Each letter is addressed to the new student who "inherits" the previous student's desk. The letter serves as an introduction to the teacher and the grade, describing what to expect during the year. Students read these letters eagerly, and there is a brief discussion of their contents.	Information about the class, etc.
8:16–8:22	The teacher briefly points out and describes procedures for some of the important features of the room, including storage shelves for supplies, drinking fountain, and bathroom facilities.	Room introduction
8:22–8:32	Then Ms. Beech explains some of the basic rules and procedures for the class, including her expectations that students will be kind to each other and raise their hands to participate in a class discussion. She explains when and how they are to sharpen their pencils, shows them the signal that she will use to get their attention, and tells them what they should do when they want her help during seatwork.	Discussion of rules and procedures

CASE STUDY 5–1: FIRST DAY OF SCHOOL (continued)

Time	Description	Activity
8:32–8:45	She explains the directions for a get-acquainted game. A ditto is distributed that presents a list of challenges, similar to a scavenger hunt. During the activity students try to find other students who fit characteristics on the list—for example, "find a student who is the same height as you are; has the same favorite television show; has the same shoe size; was born in the same month of the year; has freckles." Students are given ten minutes to work together, then the teacher leads a short class discussion.	Get-acquainted game
8:45–8:55	Following this there is a class discussion in which the teacher solicits nominations for the name of a new school mascot. The class votes on the name their class will submit.	Class discussion
8:55–8:59	The teacher presents procedures that will be followed for students using the school buses. She asks students who ride each bus to stand, and she marks these students on a seating chart of the room.	Bus procedures
8:59–9:16	Students work individually on dittos that require them to name things starting with different letters—for example, "Name a bird that starts with B," "Name a country that starts with U."	Language arts
9:16–9:26	The teacher leads a discussion and checking of the language arts activity. Students check their own work.	Checking
9:26–9:40	The teacher has students clear their desks except for a pen, and she passes out book covers and book cards. Student help distribute textbooks, one kind at a time. Students put their names in their books and they fill out a book card, using a model and information that the teacher displays on an overhead transparency. When they finish this, they look through their new books, and the teacher checks and takes up their book cards.	Book checkout
9:40–10:01	Then the teacher demonstrates how to cover a book. She works in a small group with six students who did not raise their hand when she asked who knew how to cover a book without using tape or scissors. The other students cover their own books. The class works until all students have all three new books covered.	Covering books
10:01–10:15	The teacher calls all the students to sit on the rug in a big oval. She sits with them and goes over procedures for physical education, hall passes, central office procedures, use of the phone, and bicycles on school grounds.	Discussion of school procedures
10:15–10:30	Recess	
10:30–10:35	Bathroom and water break.	

CASE STUDY 5–1: FIRST DAY OF SCHOOL (continued)

Time	Description	Activity
10:35–10:47	Students work on a handwriting sample, which will be used as a pretest for comparison with their handwriting at the end of the year. At the beginning of this activity the teacher demonstrates the heading form on the board and has all students head their papers. She then distributes a ditto containing a humorous poem, which students copy for their assignment.	Handwriting assessment
10:47–11:20	Ms. Beech leads the class through a short review lesson in their new arithmetic book. The class does the first three problems together as a group, then students do fifteen problems on their own.	
11:20–11:27	After students have finished with their seatwork, the teacher uses this occasion to present to students the procedures that they will usually use for exchanging papers to check work in class. The students then exchange papers and the class checks the fifteen problems. The papers are returned to the owners briefly, then passed forward to the teacher.	Checking
11:27–11:40	The teacher surveys students about their favorite school subjects by asking for a show of hands: Who likes spelling best, who likes arithmetic, and so on. She previews some activities in each major subject during the year and describes a field trip planned for the fall.	Preview of course content
11:40–11:45	Ms. Beech has students put their materials away and prepare to leave for lunch: She describes cafeteria rules and she tells students that when they return to the room after lunch, they are to take their seats immediately. Then she will allow them time to use the bathroom and get ready for the afternoon.	
11:45–12:15	Lunch	
12:15–12:25	After lunch, Ms. Beech has students use bathroom, sink, and drinking fountain row by row. When not engaged in this activity, students may work on their puzzle pages or rest their heads on their desks.	
12:25–12:40	The teacher introduces a creative writing and thinking activity in which students generate lists of things that fit categories listed on a handout, for example, "Name things that are made of metal." The object is to think of as many different items as possible, particularly items that are not listed by anyone else in the class. Students work individually on this assignment.	Creative writing/ thinking
12:40–1:15	Students leave the class to participate in one of their twice-a-week music classes.	
1:15–1:30	Students take a spelling pretest, which the teacher administers.	Spelling pretest

CASE STUDY 5–1: FIRST DAY OF SCHOOL (continued)

Time	Description	Activity
1:30–2:00	The class checks and then discusses the creative writing assignment they completed before going to music. The teacher uses the discussion to introduce students to a science unit on metals and minerals, which they will begin later in the week.	
2:00–2:23	The teacher passes out a ditto with a paragraph that describes facts about the city in which the students live. After reading it individually, students answer comprehension questions by filling in blanks on a ditto. The class then discusses these answers, while the students check their own work.	Social studies
2:23–2:30	Students prepare to leave for the day. The teacher makes announcements, distributes some forms for students to take home, and reminds students what to bring with them the next day.	Getting ready to go home

Second Morning of School

Time	Description	Activity
8:00–8:08	As individual students enter the room, Ms. Beech tells them to sharpen their pencils and head their papers, using the form that she has displayed on the chalkboard. While students do this, the teacher collects forms and lunch money and calls roll.	Administrative routine
8:08–8:28	She then greets the class and reads them a newspaper clipping of a story about the first day of school. She leads a discussion of the news story, brings up similarities between the classes in the story and their own class, and discusses some common feelings about the beginning of school. She also reviews some school rules and procedures, including a discussion of some problems that occurred yesterday after school. She gives the class some positive feedback about their behavior in class, and she reviews some class procedures and rules. She also discusses a new topic: What students are expected to do if they finish their work early. One option is free reading. She shows students where the magazine rack is and discusses use of the materials in it.	Discussion of rules and procedures
8:28–8:57	The teacher presents an arithmetic lesson focusing on a puzzle. The teacher and students do about half of the math puzzle as a group, then students do the remainder of the puzzle on their own.	Arithmetic puzzle
8:57–9:17	Students take a short diagnostic test on basic arithmetic operations.	Diagnostic test

CASE STUDY 5–1: SECOND MORNING OF SCHOOL (continued)

Time	Description	Activity
9:17–9:32	The teacher reads some funny poems to the class. There is a brief discussion of one of the poems, led by the teacher.	Language arts
9:32–10:15	The teacher introduces a creative writing exercise, using examples from the poems she read. Given a list of four unlikely pairs of objects, students must choose one pair and write a paragraph about how the two things are alike. Before students do this individually, the teacher presents one example and leads the class in listing similarities. Finally the teacher and class together make a list on the board of ways that things might be alike, then students work individually on their paragraphs while the teacher helps and encourages individual students.	Creative writing
10:15–10:30	Recess	
10:30–10:35	Bathroom and water break	
10:35–11:05	Ms. Beech conducts a review grammar lesson. She asks students to stand if they know what a noun is, then she asks each student standing to name one noun. If the student makes an error, he or she must sit. Then the teacher solicits the definition of a noun and reviews with the class the three common categories of person, place, or thing. She introduces a new category (idea), giving examples and leading the discussion.	Review grammar lesson
11:05–11:25	Students work individually at grammar exercises on nouns in their new textbooks.	Checking language arts seatwork
11:30–11:45	The teacher leads the class in checking their grammar exercises. Students trade papers and participate in discussing answers and checking the work.	
11:45–	Lunch.	

CASE STUDY 5–2: BEGINNING THE SCHOOL YEAR IN A PRIMARY GRADE

The First Day

Time	Description	Activity
8:00–8:10	Ms. Simpson greets the children as they enter, helps them put on their name tags, and checks the pronunciation of their names. She then instructs them to find the desk that has a laminated strip with their name on it. Ms. Simpson shows them where the crayons are and tells the children they may color a picture at their desks while they wait for everyone to arrive. She supervises the class as she waits for the last bus to arrive.	Greeting students

CASE STUDY 5–2: FIRST DAY OF SCHOOL (continued)

Time	Description	Activity
8:10–9:00	When the students are in, Ms. Simpson introduces herself to the class, then instructs the students how to answer as she checks the roll. She tells the students that the first thing they are going to do is to get to know each other. She asks the students to stand, introduce themselves, and tell one thing that they like to do.	Introductions
	Following this, she discusses the various parts of the room and explains related procedures, such as when it is all right to use the restroom or pencil sharpener. She briefly describes some of the topics they will be studying, referring to a related bulletin board. Another bulletin board has a list of school supplies they will need and examples of each. After leading a brief discussion about how supplies will be used, Ms. Simpson tells the students she will have a list of supplies for them to take home that afternoon.	Description of the room and bulletin boards
	The teacher discusses the rules that are posted: (1) We take turns. (2) We listen to others. (3) We wait quietly. (4) We walk where we want to go. (5) We respect others and their property. She encourages the students to offer the rationale and examples for each rule, and she praises them when they raise their hands to be called on.	Discussion of rules and procedures
9:00–9:15	Ms. Simpson then tells the students they are going to take a quick tour of the school. Before they line up, she explains the procedure they will use and her expectations for student behavior. When students have returned to their seats after the tour, she gives them feedback on their behavior, noting both good points and things that need improvement.	Tour of school
9:15–9:45	Ms. Simpson introduces a handwriting lesson. She goes over the instructions, being sure she has each student's attention, and passes out papers and sharpened pencils for them to practice printing their names (which students can copy from the laminated strips on their desks). After two lines of writing their names, students are instructed to copy a very simple riddle written on a transparency on the overhead projector.	Handwriting lesson
9:45–10:00	After the papers have been taken up, Ms. Simpson discusses how to come up and sit on the rug and then has the students come up by tables. She discusses the answer to the riddle students copied, then reads a story. While she is reading, she shows pictures and asks questions about the content. Then she tells the students that they will soon be lining up to go to P.E. She has the students repeat the P.E. teacher's name and reviews the rules for walking down the hall.	Story, review of hall rules

CASE STUDY 5–2: FIRST DAY OF SCHOOL (continued)

Time	Description	Activity
10:00–10:30	Students go to physical education (P.E.)	P.E.
10:30–10:35	After the students return, Ms. Simpson puts on a record for students. They are allowed to use the restroom and get a drink of water, one table at a time.	Rest break record
10:35–11:15	Ms. Simpson asks the students to take out the math books she has labeled with their names and placed under each student's desk during P.E. She reminds students to use the sharpened pencil she gave them earlier. She holds up her copy of the book and explains that each day they will tear out a sheet to work on. She shows them how this is done and then has the students do it. She circulates, giving help when needed. Then she tells the students to write signs that they see in their neighborhoods. The teacher explains the purpose of the exercise and gives instructions. They do the first part of the assignment together; then students complete the assignment individually as the teacher circulates. Students who finish quickly are given a piece of drawing paper on which to draw a sign they have seen in their neighborhood. When all students are finished, they go over the answers orally. Ms. Simpson then gives instructions for the next worksheet in their book and has the students tear the page out. After doing a couple of problems together, she instructs students to finish this worksheet and then, one at a time, bring both worksheets up to her so that she can check them. Again early finishers are instructed to work on their drawing.	Math
11:15–11:30	Ms. Simpson leads a brief summary discussion about the math assignment and then mentions other things they will be studying in math this year. She praises students for working quietly during math and asks if any students have a drawing they would like to show the class.	Math summary and sharing
11:30–11:40	Ms. Simpson discusses the lunchroom rules and procedures and describes step-by-step what the students will do. She has the students go one at a time to use the restroom, wash their hands, and get their lunches if they have them. Then they line up and go to lunch.	Discussion of lunch procedures
11:40–12:10	Lunch	Lunch
12:10–12:25	The teacher has the children put their heads down for a rest break, and she lets them use the restroom if they need to. While they are resting, the teacher plays quiet music on the record player.	Rest break

CASE STUDY 5–2: FIRST DAY OF SCHOOL (continued)

Time	Description	Activity
12:25–12:55	Ms. Simpson passes out a dittoed worksheet for use in a brief listening activity. She explains that it is very important that students know how to listen well so that they will be able to hear information and instructions. She gives each student three crayons to be used in the activity period. Then she calls out what students are supposed to do, for example, "Circle a word starting with an M with the green crayon." She circulates among the students as she calls out instructions. After they are through she appoints one person at each table to collect the papers and hand them to her when she gets to the table. After she takes up this ditto she hands out another worksheet for students to do on their own. After giving instructions, the teacher circulates as students work quietly. Then she has this ditto returned in the same way.	Listening activity and English activity
12:55–1:15	Ms. Simpson calls the students to the rug by tables. When all students are seated she compliments them on their behavior and she reviews some of the rules. Then she reads a story to the students and leads a short discussion about the story. Following this, the teacher describes a booklet they are going to be making this week, called "All about me." She describes each page that will be in the booklet and what should go on the cover. She gives each student the cover page of the booklet to illustrate and label and the first page on which students are to draw themselves doing something they like to do. Ms. Simpson says they can use their own crayons or borrow hers. They return to their seats as they get their papers.	Story introduction of booklet
1:15–2:00	While students are working at their seats, Ms. Simpson walks around supervising their work, and commenting on what a nice job they are doing.	Work on booklets
2:00–2:10	She has the students place these papers in their desks and then stand next to their chairs. She leads them in a few stretching activities and a quick game before she has a helper carry around a box to take up the crayons and pencils students used today.	Play break
2:10–2:25	Ms. Simpson reviews the day's activities by asking, "If your mom or dad ask you what you did today, what would you tell them?" She also asks questions about the rules and procedures. She reminds the students to bring their supplies tomorrow and hands a dittoed list to each student. She tells those who have already brought supplies to leave them in their desks. They are also to leave their name tags in their desks for use tomorrow. She shows them how to put their chairs on the desks so they won't fall.	Review of day's activities and rules

CASE STUDY 5-2: FIRST DAY OF SCHOOL (continued)

Time	Description	Activity
2:25–2:30	Ms. Simpson reminds the students how to line up and she calls the bus children to get in line first. She compliments the students on how well they put up their chairs, then leads them out of the room.	Getting ready to go home

Second Morning of School

Time	Description	Activity
8:00–8:07	Ms. Simpson greets the students at the door and asks them to put their supplies inside their desks, put on their name tags, and get a dittoed sheet from the front table to color.	Greeting students
8:07–8:20	When all of the students are seated, Ms. Simpson explains the beginning of class activities they will be doing every day (Pledge of Allegiance, discuss the calendar, share thoughts). After having the students rise, she repeats the words to the Pledge of Allegiance, then has the students repeat it to her. Then she has the students move to the rug to sit in a circle. She appoints a student to add today's date to the calendar (on a bulletin board next to the rug) and name the month, day, and year. Ms. Simpson explains that when someone has a birthday, they will sing Happy Birthday at this time. Then she leads the students in a brief sharing time, allowing them to talk about favorite TV shows, what they like about summer, or other suitable topics after raising their hands to be called on.	Introducing beginning of class activities
8:20–8:35	Following this discussion, Ms. Simpson reviews the rules and some of the procedures presented yesterday, calling on students to state each rule and give examples of it.	Review of rules
8:35–8:45	Then Ms. Simpson describes each of the helpers she needs and their jobs, and assigns jobs to volunteers, putting their names in slots on her helper poster.	Assigning helpers
8:45–8:50	She asks the students to go back quietly to their seats and answer as she checks the roll. She reminds students to listen as she calls the roll so they will learn other children's names.	Roll call
8:50–9:00	She asks the students to take out one pencil. While they sharpen their pencils, one table at a time, she plays a record and allows students to sing along quietly. During this activity she passes out paper to be used in a diagnostic spelling test.	Administrative routine

CASE STUDY 5–2: SECOND MORNING OF SCHOOL (continued)

Time	Description	Activity
9:00–9:10	When all pencils are sharpened, Ms. Simpson shows students how to head their papers, referring to a chart she has posted above the front chalkboard. Then she calls out the words for the test, giving a sentence using each one. After the test, she has students pass their papers to their table's student helper, who was appointed yesterday.	Diagnostic spelling test
9:10–9:40	Ms. Simpson has two appointed helpers pass out a sheet of handwriting paper and two dittos to each student. She instructs the students to copy twice (in pencil) the names of eight colors from the overhead projector, and then to complete the assignment, which calls for students to color appropriately a number of small animals on the ditto (black dog, purple fish, blue bird, etc.). When they finish they may get a sheet of drawing paper and color anything they would like.	Handwriting and color recognition
9:40–9:55	Ms. Simpson instructs students to leave their papers in the upper left-hand corner of their desks for her to look at while they are at music, then she calls the students to the rug. She does a color word recognition activity with the students, then reads a story about colors and leads a brief discussion.	Color recognition activity and story
9:55–10:30	Before having students line up to go to music, Ms. Simpson tells students the name of the music teacher and reminds students of expected behavior in the halls and in music class. Students then are asked to line up by clothing colors to go to music. While the students are in music the teacher checks the color papers and puts stickers on them.	Reminder of hall rules and music
10:30–10:35	After the students return, Ms. Simpson puts on a record. Students are allowed to use the restroom and get a drink of water.	Rest break
10:35–11:20	Ms. Simpson tells the students to put their color papers in their desks and take out their math books and a pencil. She leads them through the first part of an activity, then has them work alone to complete the page. After going over the answers, she has the students do another page from the book, again starting the assignment together. Students who finish early are instructed to get a dittoed number puzzle from the front table to work on until everyone is finished.	Math
11:20–11:35	When everyone is finished, the second math page is checked by the whole class. Then Ms. Simpson discusses some of the concepts they have been using today and what they will be doing tomorrow. All students are given a copy of the puzzle and are told to work on it while getting ready to go to lunch. The puzzles will be checked tomorrow.	Checking, math summary, puzzle

CASE STUDY 5–2: SECOND MORNING OF SCHOOL (continued)

Time	Description	Activity
11:35–11:40	Ms. Simpson reviews the lunchroom rules and gives students feedback on their behavior so far today. She also mentions something about what they will be doing in the afternoon.	Review of rules

At the end of the day all students received brief notes to take home to their parents. These notes were completed by the teacher while the students listened to a story record at the end of the day. Ms. Simpson called each student up to her, gave him or her the note and a hug. Attached to the notes were graded student papers from the first day of school.

CHAPTER SIX
MAINTAINING
GOOD STUDENT BEHAVIOR

As you have seen in the first five chapters, good classroom management depends on very careful planning of the classroom's organization, rules, procedures, and initial activities. All of this planning and preparation will pay large dividends once the students arrive because you will be ready for them. However, being ready is not sufficient to sustain good behavior throughout the year. You will need to be actively involved in maintaining student cooperation and compliance with necessary classroom rules and procedures. You cannot assume that students will behave appropriately just because you once discussed what was expected of them. In primary grades, children are in the early stages of learning "going-to-school" skills, so constant attention to prompting good behavior will be needed. Even in the intermediate grades children need teachers who encourage good behavior by using their rules, procedures, and consequences consistently.

In particular, you should not be lulled into complacency by the good behavior of your students at the beginning of the year. Most elementary classes are quiet and subdued on the first day or two of school. Without careful teacher attention to maintaining good behavior, even a class that seems to begin very well may ultimately become disruptive and difficult to control. The following brief example illustrates such a class and also suggests some of the reasons why management problems might develop.

> Ms. White carefully discussed her classroom rules and procedures with her fifth-grade class at various times on the first several class days, and students were generally well behaved. However, at the start of the second week problems are beginning to occur. While making presentations to the class, Ms. White stands at the front chalkboard in order to jot down important points. When she turns away from students to write on the board, students at the back of the room begin talking quietly among themselves. Some pass notes, throw paper wads, and leave their seats. If Ms. White reprimands students for talking during seatwork assignments, they say that they do not understand what to do and that they are just seeking help from each other. If she allows students to help each other during seatwork, before long everyone is talking, few are working, and the noise level becomes very high.
>
> At first, students raised their hands for permission to speak. Later some students called out comments, and rather than ignore the contributions, Ms. White began to accept them when they were substantive. Now more and more students are disregarding the hand-raising procedure. Class discussions and presentations are interrupted more frequently and some students have become loud and distracting. Because discussion activities do not seem to work very well, Ms. White has begun to reduce the amount of time spent on these activities and to assign more seatwork.
>
> During reading instruction, Ms. White meets with students in small groups while the rest of the class work on individual assignments. While working with the small group, Ms. White seems to be interrupted more and more frequently by seatwork students who are having problems with the assignments. At other times she has to interrupt small-group instruction to deal with misbehavior outside the group. And at the end of the small-group instruction period for reading, Ms. White frequently is dismayed to see what little progress students have made on their seatwork assignments.

Problems such as those that are occurring in Ms. White's class often have a gradual onset, developing over several weeks or even months. It is usually possible to avoid these problems, but to do so you must first understand why the problems occur and what you can do to prevent them. Because they develop gradually, the causes are not always apparent to the teacher or even to an observer unfamiliar with the history of the classroom. However, the capsule account of events in Ms. White's class suggests several reasons why things are beginning to go awry. One source of problems is that Ms. White is not *monitoring* student behavior carefully enough. Talking, inattention, and misbehavior are going undetected until the noise or commotion level is high. In addition, Ms. White is not checking student progress on assignments frequently enough. This reduces student accountability and prevents the teacher from providing the assistance that students may need to achieve the learning objectives.

A second problem is that Ms. White is being *inconsistent* in her use of procedures and in her reaction to students when they do not follow the procedures. By accepting some call-outs and by allowing noisy talk during seatwork, she invites students to continue to test the limits until the procedures finally break down.

A third problem, related to the first two, is that too many inappropriate behaviors are being *ignored.* As a result, students are unsure of behavior standards, and minor events are escalating into major disruptions involving substantial numbers of students.

These problems can be prevented or handled by the following three important guidelines:

Monitor student behavior carefully.
Be consistent in the use of procedures, rules, and consequences.
Deal with inappropriate behavior promptly.

The next three sections of the chapter discuss how these guidelines can be implemented.

MONITORING STUDENT BEHAVIOR

To monitor classroom behavior effectively, you must know first what to look for. Two categories of behavior are especially important:

Student involvement in learning activities
Student compliance with classroom rules and procedures.

Student involvement is indicated by many behaviors, including attention during presentations and discussions and satisfactory progress in seatwork and other assignments. Students' compliance with classroom rules and procedures will be easy to monitor if you have a clear set of expectations for student behavior and have communicated these to the class.

Reprinted by permission of Tribune Company Syndicate, Inc.

Monitoring student behavior during presentations requires that you stand or sit so that you can see all the faces of the students and that you scan the room frequently. Some teachers are not effective monitors of student behavior during whole-class activities because they focus their attention on a limited number of students (usually those seated in the middle rows or tables and at the front desks); other teachers "talk to the chalkboard." In either case the teacher does not have a very clear perception of overall student response to the presentation nor is he or she fully aware of what may be occurring at the periphery of the classroom. During your presentations, therefore, try to move around and develop "active eyes." If you notice a commotion involving several students and you have no idea of what is going on, this is a sign that you have not been monitoring closely enough.

When instructing a small group of students while the remainder of the class is engaged in individual seatwork, be sure to sit where you have an unobstructed view of all the students. Don't become so absorbed in working with the small group that you lose track of the other children. Look up frequently and be alert for problems. After finishing with one group, circulate around the room and provide needed assistance before calling the next small group for instruction.

When students are working on individual assignments and you are not instructing a group, you should monitor the class by circulating around the classroom and checking each student's progress periodically. You will of course help students who request assistance; however, you should not just "chase hands" or you will not be aware of the progress of other students. It is very difficult to monitor student progress on assignments from your desk or from any other fixed location, so spend as little time in one place as possible. If you must work at your desk for a time, get up periodically and circulate around the room, looking at each student's work. If you must spend a long time (more than a minute or two) helping an individual student, avoid doing it at the student's desk unless you can monitor the rest of the class from that position. If the student's seat is in the middle of the room, for instance, half of the class will be behind you. In such a case call the student to a small-group work table, to your desk, or to some other location from which you can easily see all the students. Finally, when you work at your desk or at any other location, don't let students congregate around the area. They will obstruct your view of the class, and they will probably distract students seated nearby. Instead, call students to you one at a time.

A monitoring technique that is effective in getting everyone started on their seatwork is to begin the work as a whole-group activity. That is, have students get out the necessary materials (be sure to look for these on the students' desks), head their papers, and then do the first exercise, problem, or question under your direction. Then check and discuss the first item as a group. Using this approach, you can easily scan the room to be sure that everyone has begun and check on whether students understand what to do.

A critical monitoring task is checking assignments. Collect them regularly and look them over, even when students do the checking in class. Keep your grade book current so you will be able to detect students who skip assignments. If you teach an intermediate grade class, you may give a long-term assignment. If so, be sure to check progress regularly. You may even give a grade or assign points toward a grade at these progress checks.

CONSISTENCY

The dictum "be consistent" has been repeated more frequently than the Pledge of Allegiance. It is still worth some discussion, though, because its meaning is not always clear. In the classroom *consistency* means retaining the same expectations for appropriate behavior in an activity at all times and for all students. For example, if students are expected to work silently during seatwork activities on Monday, the same procedure is in effect on Tuesday, Wednesday, and the rest of the week. Penalties should also be applied consistently. For example, if the penalty for missing assignments is losing one's place on an honor list, the teacher must make sure that all students who skip assignments receive the penalty. This procedure should be followed even when it is inconvenient to administer it or in spite of the pleading of individual students that an exception be made. Obvious inconsistency in the use of procedures or in the application of penalties will cause confusion about what is acceptable behavior. Students will frequently "test the limits" by not following the procedure or by repeating whatever behavior was to have evoked the penalty. These events can rapidly escalate and force the teacher either to abandon the procedure or to tolerate high levels of inappropriate behavior. Because neither outcome is desirable, it is best to avoid the problem by learning to be consistent from the start. Of course, it is not possible to be totally consistent; there will be occasions when the most reasonable course of action will be to make an exception to a rule or procedure. Thus, a deadline for an assignment may be extended when a student has a valid reason, or some procedures might be ignored during an emergency. Note that using certain procedures routinely for some activities but not for others is not inconsistent. For example, you may require that no students leave their seats without permission during discussions or presentations but you may allow them to get materials, sharpen pencils, or turn in papers as needed without permission during seatwork. As long as you have differentiated between the activities when you explain the procedures to the students, no problems should arise.

Undesirable inconsistency usually arises from three sources. First, the procedures or rules as presented are not reasonable, workable, or appropriate. Second, the teacher fails to monitor students closely and detects only a fraction of the inappropriate behavior. This creates the appearance of inconsistency. Finally, the teacher may not feel strongly enough about the procedure or rule to enforce it or to use the associated penalty. If you find yourself caught in an inconsistency that is becoming a problem, your alternatives are:

1. Reteach the procedure to the class. Take a few minutes to discuss the problem with the class and to reiterate your desire that they follow the procedure. Then enforce it.

2. Modify the procedure or consequence and then reintroduce and use it.

3. Abandon the procedure or consequence, and possibly substitute another in its place.

Your choice of the alternatives depends on circumstances and the importance of the item to your classroom management system.

PROMPT MANAGEMENT OF INAPPROPRIATE BEHAVIOR

Inappropriate behavior must be handled promptly to keep it from continuing and spreading. Behaviors that you should be concerned about include lack of involvement in learning activities, prolonged inattention or work avoidance, and obvious violations of classroom rules and procedures. It is *not* a good idea to ignore such behavior: Prolonged inattention will make it difficult for the students to learn and to be able to complete assignments; violations of rules and failure to follow procedures create many problems we have already discussed. These behaviors should be dealt with directly but without overreaction. A calm, reasoned tone or approach will be more productive and less likely to lead to confrontation. The following alternatives are recommended.

Four Ways to Manage Inappropriate Behavior

1. When the student is off task—that is, not working on an assignment— redirect his or her attention to the task. "Sammy, you should be writing now," or "Cynthia, the assignment is to complete all the problems on the page." Check the students' progress shortly thereafter to make sure they are continuing to work.

2. Make eye contact with or move closer to the student. Use a signal, such as a finger to the lips or a head shake to prompt the appropriate behavior. Monitor until the student complies.

3. If the student is not following a procedure correctly, simply reminding the student of the correct procedure may be effective. You can either state the correct procedure or ask the student if he or she remembers it.

4. Ask or tell the student to stop the inappropriate behavior. Then monitor until it stops and the student begins constructive activity.

Sometimes it is inconvenient or would interrupt an activity to use these procedures immediately. If the behavior is not disruptive or is not likely to spread to other students, make a mental note of the problem and continue the activity until a more appropriate time occurs. Then tell the student you saw what was happening and discuss what the appropriate behavior should have been.

The four procedures outlined above are easy to use, cause little interruption of class activities, and enable students to correct their behavior. However, if a student persists in an unacceptable behavior, then some other alternatives should be used. If the rest of the class is working appropriately and does not need your immediate attention, then a brief talk with the student may be sufficient. If that doesn't settle the matter, or if an immediate conference is not desirable or feasible, stop the child's behavior and assess whatever penalty is appropriate. Some teachers use a "time-out" desk or chair as a holding area for erring students; others have students wait outside the classroom until time can be found for a conference. Note that the four procedures apply to relatively minor forms of misbehavior. More severe transgressions (such as open defiance or fighting) are discussed in the last section of this chapter, "Special Problems."

When to Ignore

Some inappropriate behaviors are of such short duration or are so insignificant that they can be safely ignored. Indeed, to do otherwise would give them undesirable attention and interfere unnecessarily with your helping other students or with the flow of the lesson. You can ignore inappropriate behavior when it meets the following criteria:

1. It is of short duration and not likely to persist or spread.
2. It is a minor deviation.
3. Reacting to it would interrupt a lesson or call attention to the behavior.

Examples of behaviors that meet these criteria include occasional callouts during discussions, brief whispering among students during a presentation, and short periods of inattentiveness, perhaps accompanied by visual wandering or daydreaming. There is no point in worrying about such trivial behaviors as long as they are not disruptive; they don't significantly affect student cooperation or involvement in learning activities. To react to them would consume too much of your energy, interrupt your lessons constantly, and detract from your classroom climate.

SPECIAL PROBLEMS

Children sometimes behave in ways that require stronger measures than those described in the preceding sections. Some such behaviors include: rudeness toward the teacher, chronic avoidance of work, fighting, other aggressive behavior, and defiance or hostility toward the teacher. While these behaviors are not pleasant to contemplate, they are an inevitable result of close contact with up to thirty children for long periods of time. Fortunately, few teachers encounter these behaviors in large amounts. Regardless of their frequency, you should be aware of ways to cope with them if they should occur.

Before discussing each type of problem, some general guidelines applicable to aggressive behaviors will be considered. You should think of coping with these behaviors in two phases: the immediate response and a long-range strategy. At the time you encounter the behavior, your immediate concern will be to bring it to a halt with a minimum of further disruption. Because these behaviors are annoying and frequently arouse anxiety or anger, you will need to be careful not to exacerbate the problem. Stay calm and avoid overreaction. You can tell the student how you feel, but avoid an argument or an emotional confrontation. Then you will be in a better position to deal with the student and his or her problem. Long-range considerations are to prevent a recurrence of the behavior and to help the student learn a more constructive means of dealing with others. Preventing a recurrence of the behavior is best accomplished (1) by finding out what triggered the incident and dealing with the cause if possible, and (2) by having a predictable classroom environment, with reasonable and consistently used rules, procedures, and consequences. Such classrooms rarely have large amounts of aggressive behaviors. Helping a child acquire better behavior may require dealing with the student on an individual basis over a period of time. The extent to which this goal is feasible is of course limited by many factors, including your time constraints and the severity of the child's problem. In dealing with chronic problems, the child's parents and professionals such as the school counselor, a special education resource teacher, or the principal may be able to assist you.

In the discussion below some suggestions for handling different types of behavior are presented.

Rudeness toward the teacher.   Rudeness may take the form of sassy backtalk, arguing, crude remarks, or gesturing. An important consideration of this type of behavior is not to overreact or argue with the student. Frequently, the child is using such behavior as a means of getting attention either from you or from peers, so you should avoid getting yourself trapped in a power struggle. To some extent your response will depend on the degree of rudeness. In borderline cases the student may not even realize that a comment was offensive. A reasonable first reaction is to inform the student that the behavior is not acceptable and to refer to a general classroom rule such as "respect others" or "be polite." If the incident is repeated or if the original comment was intentionally rude, then some type of penalty should be used. In the case of obnoxious behavior that disrupts the class or that persists, the student should be isolated from the other students or sent to the school office and not allowed to return until he or she agrees to behave appropriately. Most schools have a standard policy for dealing with extreme cases, and you should use whatever procedures have been established.

Chronic avoidance of work.   You may have students who frequently do not complete assigned work. Sometimes they fail to complete assignments early in the school year; more often a student will begin to skip assignments occasionally and then with increasing regularity until he or she is habitually failing to do the assigned work. This behavior can be minimized by a carefully planned accountability system (review Chapter Three for details). However, even in classrooms with a strong accountability system, some students may still avoid work.

It is much easier and better for the teacher to correct this problem before the student gets so far behind that failure is almost certain. In order to be in a position to take early action, you must collect and check student work frequently and also maintain good records. When you note a student who has begun to miss assignments, you can talk with him or her, seeking further information to help identify the problem, and then take corrective action. If the student is simply unable to do the assigned work, you should provide appropriate assistance or modify the assignments for that student. If the student feels overwhelmed by the assignments, break up the assignments into parts whenever possible. Have the student complete the first part of the assignment within a specific time (perhaps five or ten minutes), then check to see that it has been done. A bonus of a few minutes of free time at the end of the period can be offered for completion of the portion within the time limit or for working steadily without prodding.

If ability is not the problem, then in addition to talking with the student, the following procedures can be used. Call the student's parents and discuss the situation with them. Often the home can supply the extra support needed to help motivate the student. A simple penalty of requiring that the student remain after school until assignments have been completed can prove effective. If the student rides a bus, you won't be able to use the procedure, of course, without making special arrangements with the parents. Anytime the child is likely to be detained for more than a few minutes, you should alert the parents ahead of time. Another procedure that can be used when the parents are cooperative is for the child to take home daily a list of incomplete assignments and all books or materials needed to complete the work.

Be sure not to soften the negative consequences of repeated failure to complete work by giving such students higher grades than they have earned. To do so just teaches them to avoid responsibility. Finally, try to provide added incentives for good effort and completed work. Set up a reward system (see Chapter Four) that encourages the children to do their best.

Fighting.   Fighting is less likely to occur in classrooms than on the playground, in the cafeteria, or in some other area of the school. In the elementary grades you can usually stop a fight without undue risk of injury. (If for some reason you cannot intervene directly, you should of course alert other teachers and administrators so that action can be taken.) When you do intervene, first give a loud verbal command to stop. This alone may stop the fight; it will at least alert the combatants that a referee has arrived. Then separate the fighters. Keep them apart until help arrives, and get them away from the crowd that's sure to have gathered.

Your school will undoubtedly have a procedure to deal with fighting; you should carry it out. Students may be questioned by the princi-

"... and suddenly there were teachers
all over the place!"

© 1968 by Bill Knowlton. Reprinted from *Classroom Chuckles* published by Scholastic
Book Services, a Division of Scholastic, Inc., by permission of Bill Knowlton.

pal, who may call the student's home, arrange a conference, and mete
out any prescribed penalty.

If school policy leaves the teacher with wide discretion in following up on such incidents, then you should decide on your procedures. It
is generally best to arrange a cooling-off period. If you cannot find
someone to supervise your class, let the fighters wait in separate areas
or in the school office. Older children can cool off by writing their ver-
sion of how the fight started. If you do not know what started the fight,
try to find out from uninvolved students. As soon as you have an opportunity, meet with the offenders and get each one's point of view. The
conference should focus on the inappropriateness of fighting and the
need to resolve problems in other ways rather than on accusations or
personal criticism. Help each student understand the other's point-of-
view so that they have a basis for better communication. Finally, stress
the importance of cooperativeness and friendliness toward one another.
During the next day or two watch for any indications of residual hostility. If the issue seems not to have been resolved, you should follow up by
contacting the children's parents, discussing the matter with your principal, and/or talking with the students again.

Other aggressive behavior.   Aggressive behavior toward other
students is not confined to open fighting. Name calling, overbearing
bossiness or rudeness toward other students, and physically aggressive
but "playful" pushing, shoving, or slapping are examples of other forms
of aggressive behavior found in the classroom. Such behavior should be

treated just like rudeness toward the teacher. You should tell offending students that such behavior is not acceptable, even if they are just "fooling around." It can easily escalate. Refer to whatever class rule fits the situation, such as "respect others." Give no more than one warning and then assess whatever penalty is appropriate. Students engaged in such behavior should be separated and seated apart if they give any indication of intending to persist.

Defiance or hostility toward the teacher.   Defiance or hostility is understandably very threatening to teachers. The teacher feels, and rightfully so, that if he or she allows the student to get away with it, the behavior may continue and other students will be more likely to react in the same way. The student, who has provoked a confrontation, usually publicly, feels that backing down would cause a loss of face in front of peers. The best way to deal with such an event is to try to defuse it. This can be done by keeping it private and handling it individually with the student, if possible. If it occurs during a lesson and is not very extreme, deal with it by trying to depersonalize the event and avoid a power struggle. "This is taking time away from the lesson. I will discuss it with you in a few minutes when I have time." If the student does not accept the opportunity you have provided and presses the confrontation further, then instruct the student to leave the room and wait in the hall. After the student has had time to cool off, give your class something to do and discuss the problem with the student.

When discussing the incident, you should remain objective. Do not engage in arguments with the student. Point out that the behavior was not acceptable, state the penalty clearly, and implement it. Listen to the student's point of view and respond to it. If you are not sure how to respond, say that you will think about it and discuss it later. However, you should still administer the penalty.

In an extreme (and rare) case, the student may be totally uncooperative and refuse to keep quiet or to leave the room. If this happens, you can escort the student from the room yourself or, when dealing with an older larger student, send another student to the office for assistance. In most cases, however, as long as you stay calm and refuse to get into a power struggle with the student, the student will accept the opportunity to cool down.

SUGGESTED ACTIVITIES

Each of the two short paragraphs below describes a common problem situation in an elementary classroom. After reading each, review the contents of this chapter and think about some specific strategies you might use to deal with the problem. You might also discuss both problem cases with other teachers or put together "brainstorming" lists of suggestions for addressing each problem. Because of the limited information provided in the descriptions, many alternative causes of action are potentially valid, so do not be concerned with finding a single correct solution. Instead, generate a variety of possibilities to choose from. Then compare your lists with the suggestions in the activity key in Appendix B.

Problem 6–1: Improving Class Behavior

Ms. Johnson is concerned because no matter how hard she tries to follow through with classroom behavior requirements, her students continue to talk to each other, call out to her, and behave in ways that they know are not acceptable to her. Within one typical ten-minute morning segment, she wrote the names of five students on the board for talking after being warned to stop several times; she sent one child to stand in the time-out corner for wandering around and bothering other students; she warned one girl twice about calling out answers; and she threatened to send two boys to the office for running in the classroom. What could Ms. Johnson do to improve behavior of students in her class?

Problem 6–2: Impulsive Students

Mr. Wilson feels that he has a class of good students, with two exceptions. Jimmy never seems to stay at this desk. He wanders, takes constant trips to the pencil sharpener or wastepaper basket, dances around the classroom, bothers other children, and generally stirs up the class. Richard is also disruptive, constantly calling out answers and "smart" remarks to the teacher and to other students. The class is regularly either stirred up and annoyed by Jimmy or distracted and laughing at Richard. How can Mr. Wilson help these two students improve their behavior?

CHAPTER SEVEN
ORGANIZING
AND CONDUCTING
INSTRUCTION

The way in which instruction is organized and conducted can have a significant impact on your overall classroom management effectiveness. Carefully planned and executed instructional activities contribute to classroom management by conserving time, by increasing student engagement and success in learning activities, and by reducing boredom, frustration, confusion, and failure. This chapter will focus on recommendations for designing activities to maximize student learning and involvement and for conducting clear, comprehensible instruction. It is not intended as a substitute for a thorough treatment of teaching methodology in particular subjects. However, the tasks of communicating instruction clearly, arranging activities to involve students, and providing practice and feedback are common to many subjects in the elementary school curriculum. It is these generic features of instruction that this chapter will describe and illustrate.

ORGANIZING INSTRUCTIONAL ACTIVITIES

When teachers choose instructional activities for their classes, they consider several things. Primarily, they think about whether an activity will lead to student learning, but they also must consider whether the activity will maintain student involvement. The sequence of activities and the amounts of time spent in the various subjects in the curriculum must also be weighed. Such considerations lead many elementary teachers to schedule reading and at least some language arts activities for the first two hours or so of the morning. These activities usually require sustained effort and often involve a combination of small-group and seatwork formats. Student involvement in these activities would be more difficult to maintain later in the day when students are less alert and more fatigued.

It is wise to establish a daily schedule with specific times allocated to different subjects. Doing so will help you remain conscious of time so that you do not shortchange subjects taught later in the day. Furthermore, students will be better able to pace their own work if they know what schedule will be followed. When you plan your schedule, try to arrange some change-of-pace activities to follow periods of sustained effort or intense concentration. For example, you might schedule recess, art, physical education, or music following the reading/language arts activities if possible. If you cannot schedule such activities conveniently, then at least give students a brief break and lead them in exercises, a song or two, or just give them a little time to stand and stretch.

When you begin to plan your daily schedule, you may find that your school district has established guidelines for the amounts of time to be allotted to different subjects. Also, special teachers may be assigned to teach a particular subject for certain days and times of the week. Thus you may find that your class will be taught physical education on Tuesday and Thursday from 1:30 to 2:00 and will have music on Monday and Wednesday from 10:30 to 11:00. Obviously your schedule will need to be set accordingly.

Even though much of your planning will focus on the organization of daily activities within each subject, you should also keep in mind a broader perspective. You need to know what knowledge and skills students are expected to acquire in your grade, and what units, topics, or textbook chapters are typically included in each subject. Examine the teacher's edition of your textbooks, preview each major section, and note statements of overall objectives and the scope and sequence of the content. Forming an impression of the content experts' views of a subject and identifying reasonable expectations for your grade level will be helpful when deciding on course objectives and adequate coverage of topics. Other useful sources of information on particular age and grade levels may be found in school district or state education agency curriculum guides, courses and books on instructional methods, and yearbooks of national teacher organizations in particular subjects. Finally, other teachers at your grade level and instructional coordinators or

supervisors can provide helpful suggestions on the scope and topical sequence for particular subjects.

Types of Instructional Activities

For each subject that you teach, you will choose a series of activities to
help students acquire skills or new learning, practice the skills, consolidate and extend their knowledge, and receive feedback about their performance. In this section the major types of instructional activities used
to reach these goals are described. Then several concepts are discussed
that are critical to the management of activities: sequencing, pacing,
and transitions.

Content development. During content development activities
the teacher presents new information, elaborates or extends a concept
or principle, conducts a demonstration, shows how to perform a skill, or
describes how to solve a problem. Although teachers sometimes present
content to students individually or in small groups, whole class presentation is often the major vehicle for introducing and teaching content
objectives. In our discussion we will assume that the content development activity is taking place in a whole-class format. During content
development activities the teacher takes an active role, focused on
bringing students into contact with the instructional content. The fact
that the teacher is active, however, does not mean that the students are
passive. Student involvement in the development of the lesson should
be encouraged. Teacher questions are used for this purpose, allowing
the teacher to check student understanding, to encourage students to
contribute to the steps in problem solving, to apply concepts or principles, or to analyze ideas being presented. In addition to questioning for
comprehension, it is usually a good idea to have students do sample
problems or demonstrate their grasp of the skills being taught in other
ways. This can be done as a whole-class activity so that the teacher
gains a clear understanding of the degree to which students are following the content development. Thus content development activities are
characteristically interactive. Because of this activity's importance for
effective instruction, it will be described in more detail in this chapter's
final section on clarity.

Seatwork. In this activity students engage in assignments that
provide practice or review of previously presented material. In the
upper elementary grades, that portion of the seatwork assignment not
completed in class often becomes a homework assignment unless the
materials or resources needed to finish it are only available in the
classroom. (Procedures for seatwork have been discussed in Chapter
Two, and the reader should refer to it if additonal review is needed.)

"You mean we have to process all that data?"

Seatwork is useful mainly for consolidating or applying prior learning through practice rather than for learning *new* content. For that reason and also because it is difficult to maintain student involvement in lengthy seatwork activities, periods of student seatwork should be moderate in length whenever possible. When the seatwork period is likely to be long (e.g., more than 20 minutes), you should provide some variety. If students must engage in seatwork for very long, as they are often expected to do when you are working with other students in small groups, give two or three short assignments on different topics rather than one very long assignment.

A form of seatwork, which we will call *classwork,* is often used in conjunction with content development activities and before giving students a more extensive seatwork assignment. In classwork activities the teacher selects a small number of exercises, problems, or questions which review the material presented in the content development activity and preview the seatwork assignment. Students are asked to complete the exercises individually, then the teacher has students check and review the work as a whole class or group. This enables the teacher to check immediately for student understanding and ability to do the assignment, and allows him or her to provide quick feedback or reteaching if necessary.

Checking.   In this activity students check their seatwork or homework, or they may exchange papers and check one another's work. The activity is appropriate only when the judgment of correctness can easily be made. Checking provides quick feedback to students, and it allows the teacher to identify and discuss common errors on assignments. Careful monitoring during checking is important to be sure that students are doing it correctly. When student checking is used, you should collect the students' papers and examine them, even when you record grades in class, in order to keep abreast of student progress and problems.

Recitation.   This activity is a question-and-answer sequence in which the teacher asks questions, usually of a factual nature, and accepts or corrects student responses. The sequence of question/answer/ evaluation is repeated frequently, with many students being asked to respond until a body of content has been covered. In effect, a recitation is a form of checking that is done orally. It can be used as a skill drill or to review student understanding of a previous lesson or assigned reading. It can also be used to check spelling, knowledge of vocabulary words, or other verbal learning.

Discussion.   Discussion is used to encourage students to evaluate events, topics, or results; to clarify the basis for their opinions; to help them become aware of other points of view, or to help them improve their oral expression skills. Sometimes discussions are begun with a recitation activity in which the facts of the content to be discussed are reviewed. Compared to a recitation, however, discussion questions are more likely to elicit the students' judgments, impressions, ideas, and opinions; also, teachers are less likely to evaluate the student responses directly. Instead, students are encouraged to express themselves, to examine their opinions and beliefs, and to understand other perspectives. The teacher's role then becomes one of encouraging, clarifying, and using student ideas, rather than evaluating their correctness. When using a discussion format, careful planning of questions is needed. Students also should be made aware of your ground rules for participation (for example, raise hands, listen carefully, respect each person's right to express themselves). Discussion activities are difficult to sustain in the primary grades for very long; even in the intermediate grades, discussion should be limited to very short times (about ten minutes) until you have an idea of what you and your classes can handle.

Student work in groups.   This activity should not be confused with small-group instruction, which is described below. During student work in groups, two or more students work together on a task that requires their cooperation. This activity might be used for drills on new vocabulary words or spelling, work on a science or social studies project, reviewing for a test, preparing a group report, or building a display or other art project. Small groups work best when goals are clear and the steps to achieving them are understood by the students. Small groups should be carefully monitored to be sure they are on track and to provide appropriate assistance.

Small-group instruction.   In this activity the teacher works with small groups of students, one group at a time, while the remainder of the class works on seatwork assignments. This mode of instruction is most commonly used for reading and is frequently used for mathematics instruction as well. Its purpose, of course, is to accommodate a wide range of student ability in basic skill subjects. Because small-group instruction is used so extensively for basic skills, we will describe its features in detail.

A critical thing to note about small group instruction is that two different activities occur simultaneously: a teacher-led group and individual seatwork. Because the teacher is actively involved with the small group, it is more difficult for him or her to monitor the behavior of students doing seatwork and give them assistance. And because students may need to be engaged in seatwork for a long period of time, very careful planning and extra effort will be required to keep them involved in their work.

The first step in setting up effective small-group instruction is to set the stage for the seatwork activities. Give directions for the seatwork to the whole class at once, including the following: instructions for each seatwork assignment, a description of materials that will be needed, and to help students pace their work, a suggested time for completing each activity. This list of seatwork assignments should also be posted or written on the chalkboard. It would be wise to check whether students understand the directions by asking students in each group to review them before beginning the seatwork.

Before calling the first group, monitor the beginning of seatwork for a short time. After you are certain that students have started, signal the first group orally or with a bell. During your work with the small group, monitor seatwork students by scanning the room frequently. If you observe inappropriate behavior that is interfering with seatwork, try to stop it with eye contact or some nonverbal signal, by calling the student's name once, or by reminding the wayward worker of what he or she should be doing. A "time-out" desk near you can also be used for a student who persists in misbehavior: You can then signal such a student to go to the desk for a while, without your having to leave the group.

Another problem to consider is how students needing help on a seatwork activity can obtain it without interrupting the teacher. Some teachers tell students to skip work they cannot do and go onto another activity until the teacher is available to assist them. Others allow students to help each other, or they assign a few students (perhaps one for each table or group) the role of helper. Finally, students can sign up on the chalkboard or on a clipboard sheet to indicate the need for assistance when you are available. If you must leave the small group to help a student or to deal with a problem, be sure to give students in the group something to do. A student in the group may be able to lead the activity for a short time.

When work with one small group has been completed, the next group should *not* be called immediately. Instead, take the opportunity to check the progress of the students who will be continuing in seatwork and help them with any problems they have encountered. Students who were off-task during seatwork can also be given delayed feedback at this time. Be sure to encourage and give positive feedback to students who are working. The students who have left the small group and are returning to seatwork should also be monitored to be sure they begin their activity promptly. Then signal the next group to come for instruction.

In the preceding discussion of activities, each activity was treated as a discrete event; in practice, activities are often combined. For example, content development activities may be blended with discussion, recitation, or classwork. If you find that using some mixture of activities is more suitable for your lesson goals than planning separate activities, by all means pursue the lesson structure that best accomplishes your objectives.

Arranging Activities Within a Lesson

In any given subject, lessons usually consist of a series of activities. A common activity sequence is:

> Checking or recitation
> Content development
> Classwork
> Seatwork

The first activity allows the previous day's seatwork assignment or homework to be corrected. If there was no homework, the teacher leads a review of prior content important for the day's lesson. During the content development activity, new content or skills are taught. Following this, a short classwork activity is used to review the new content and to preview the seatwork assignment. Then practice is provided during the seatwork activities.

The problem with that sequence is that it requires that the presentation of lesson content and the practice period each be handled in two, usually lengthy, segments. A variation of the sequence that accommodates more complex content and that does not demand as much sustained student attention is:

Checking or recitation
Content development
Classwork or seatwork, usually brief, with checking
Content development
Classwork, usually brief
Seatwork

This sequence allows the teacher to divide the lesson content into two parts, with practice and feedback following the first content development activity. Teaching new content in two parts with an intervening practice period will help students consolidate learning from the first part before they are asked to contend with the new learning required in the second part of the lesson. The sequence also allows the teacher to check student understanding and to provide prompt feedback before moving on to more complex content. Furthermore, when individual activities are divided into shorter segments, student attention is usually easier to maintain. A problem with the sequence is that it produces more transition points and thus greater potential for student disengagement. Usually these transitions can be managed without difficulty, however, because student movement, new materials, or drastically changed lesson focus will not be required in the content development-classwork-seatwork cycle. Thus the various activities will blend together, usually without conspicuous transitions.

Pacing

In content development activities, pacing refers to the fit between the rate of presentation and the students' ability to comprehend it. In seatwork activities, pacing refers to the time students have to complete tasks relative to task demands. Appropriate pacing requires that adequate time be available for all the activities. The teacher must also be aware of student comprehension so that the rate of presentation or the task can be modified as needed. Maintaining an appropriate pace requires good planning, an awareness of time during the lesson, and the self-discipline to reserve adequate time for each activity. Staying abreast of student comprehension requires careful monitoring of student progress, especially during content development activities. Frequent questions, written work samples, and demonstrations of performance by students should be used as checks on student understanding.

Pacing can be affected by interruptions. Students can interrupt an activity by getting out of their seats, being disruptive, inappropriate calling out, or coming up to the teacher. Environmental conditions such as noise in the hallway, poor room arrangement, or visitors can intrude into the lesson, sometimes with great frequency. Such problems can best be handled by taking preventive measures: establishing and enforcing appropriate rules and procedures to manage student behavior and taking action to adjust or to eliminate chronic external distractions. Teachers themselves are sometimes responsible for interruptions when they do not have materials and other lesson props available when needed, and when they stop and start the lesson, insert irrelevancies, are unclear, or present lesson content unsystematically. Careful lesson planning will help prevent these problems, as will attention to other suggestions for approving clarity (discussed in the last section of this chapter).

TRANSITIONS

The interval between any two activities is a transition. Several management problems can occur during transitions, including long delays before starting the next activity and high levels of inappropriate or disruptive behavior. Transition problems can be caused by a lack of readiness by the teacher or the students for the next activity, unclear student expectations about appropriate behavior during transitions, and faulty procedures for transitions. Following are some examples of transition problems along with some suggested ways of correcting them.

Transition Problem	*Suggested Solution*
Students talk loudly at the beginning of the day. The teacher is interrupted while checking attendance, and the start of content activities is delayed.	Establish a beginning-of-day routine, and clearly state your expectations for student behavior at the beginning of the day.
Students talk too much during transitions, especially after a seatwork assignment has been given but before they've begun working on it. Many students do not start their seatwork activity for several minutes.	Be sure students know what the assignment is, post it where they can easily see it. Work as a whole class on the first several seatwork exercises so that all students begin the lesson successfully and at the same time. Watch what students do during the transition and urge them along when needed.

Transition Problem (continued)	*Suggested Solution* (continued)
During the last afternoon activity students quit working well before the end; they then begin playing around and leave the room in a mess.	Establish an end-of-day routine so that students continue their work until the teacher gives a signal to begin preparations to leave; then instruct students to help straighten up the room.
Whenever the teacher attempts to move the students from one activity into another, a number of students don't make the transition, but continue working on the preceding activity. This delays the start of the next activity or results in confusion.	Give students a few minutes notice before an activity is scheduled to end. At the end of the activity students should put all the materials from it away and get out any needed materials for the next activity. Monitor the transition to make sure that all students complete it; do not start next activity until students are ready.
As the teacher gives directions during a transition, many students do not pay attention and continue to work, put their materials away, or get out new materials.	Don't try to give instructions *during* a transition except to individual students. Instead, give the whole class instructions before the transition begins. Don't begin explaining the new activity or presenting content until everyone is ready and listening.
A few students always seem to be slowpokes during transitions, delaying the rest of the class.	Don't hold up the rest of the class for one or two students. Go ahead and start, but be sure to monitor the dawdlers in later transitions to find out why they are having trouble. Then give them individual feedback and close supervision.
Students frequently leave their seats to socialize, come up to the teacher to ask questions, use the bathroom, go to the trash basket, or wander around the room during transitions.	Define appropriate behavior during transitions more clearly and explain the rationale for limiting student behavior during these times. Monitor students, and be sure to establish procedures to handle out-of-seat behavior.
The teacher delays the beginning of activities to look for materials, finish attendance reporting, pass back or collect papers, or chat with individual students while the rest of the class waits.	Have materials organized ahead of time, and once transitions begin, avoid doing anything that interferes with your ability to monitor and direct students.

The preceding items summarize the major problems that occur in classrooms at and around transition times. If you feel that your class is wasting time or if you are having difficulty keeping control during transitions, then a look at the suggested solutions may prove helpful.

CLARITY[1]

Communicating information and directions in a clear, comprehensible manner is a very important teaching skill. Clear instruction helps students learn faster and more successfully; it also helps students understand your directions and expectations for behavior more readily. Although clarity is important in all classroom activities, it is crucial during content development, the time when nearly all new subject matter is introduced and taught. This section will focus on ways to improve clarity during this critical portion of your lessons.

Clear instruction results from several factors: The organization of information into a coherent sequence, the use of an adequate number of illustrations or examples, precision and concreteness of expression, keeping in touch with student comprehension, and providing enough practice to insure mastery. The following chart illustrates some of the many ways teachers can be both clear and unclear in their instruction.

Poor Clarity	*Good Clarity*
1. Communicating Lesson Objectives	
Not describing the lesson's purpose or what students are expected to learn	Stating goals or major objectives
Not calling students' attention to main points, ideas, or concepts	Telling students what they will be accountable for knowing or doing
	Emphasizing major ideas
	Reviewing key points or objectives at the end of the lesson
2. Presenting Information Systematically	
Presenting information out of sequence, skipping important points, or backtracking	Outlining the lesson sequence and sticking to it
Inserting extraneous information, comments, or trivia into the lesson	Sticking to the topic, holding back on complexities until the main idea is developed
Moving from one topic to another without warning	Summarizing previous points, clearly delineating major transitions between ideas or topics
Presenting too much complex information at once or giving directions too quickly	Breaking complex content into manageable portions, giving step-by-step directions, and checking for understanding before proceeding
Not leaving sufficient time to cover each aspect of the lesson	Maintaining an efficient pace in early activities so that ample time remains for later ones
3. Avoiding Vagueness	
Presenting concepts without concrete examples	Providing a variety of apt examples
Using overly complex vocabulary	Using words students understand; defining new vocabulary terms

[1]The authors appreciate the suggestions of Barak Rosenshine for the organization and content of this section.

Poor Clarity (continued)

Overusing negative phrases (e.g., not all insects, not many people, not very happy)

Being ambiguous or indefinite: maybe, perhaps, sort of correct, more or less right, you know, right most of the time, not always

4. Checking for Understanding

Assuming that everyone understands without verification

Moving to the next topic because time is short or no students ask questions

Not calling on slower students; relying only on feedback from a few volunteers

5. Providing for Practice and Feedback

Not assigning classwork or homework

Giving assignments that cover only a portion of the content

Not checking, reviewing, or discussing students' assigned work

Good Clarity (continued)

Being specific and direct (e.g., the beetles, one third of the people, discouraged)

Being specific, precise, referring to the concrete object, stating what is and is not correct and why

Asking questions or obtaining work samples to be sure students are ready to move on

Asking students to summarize main points to verify comprehension

Reteaching unclear parts

Checking everyone's understanding

Being sure students have adequate practice so that critical objectives are mastered

Reviewing assignments to be sure that all of the lesson's skills are reinforced

Checking work regularly, reexplaining needed concepts, reteaching when appropriate

Teaching Clearly

As the preceding examples illustrate, teachers can do many things to enhance—or detract from—the clarity of lessons. Following are some specific suggestions that you can apply to different aspects of your lessons and their planning.

Reprinted by permission of Tribune Company Syndicate, Inc.

Planning.   Organize your lesson parts into a coherent sequence. If the lesson is complex, write down or outline the main components. Review the unit and lesson in the teacher's edition of your textbook(s). Pay careful attention to suggestions for lesson development and activities. Study the exercises, questions, problems, and other activities in the textbook and decide which items would provide appropriate review of lesson objectives. Note examples, demonstrations, and key questions and activities to use in the development of the main concepts. If some items in the seatwork assignment go well beyond the lesson scope, don't assign them as classwork or homework until you can teach the necessary content. If the content is not essential and you do not plan to teach it later, then assign such items only as enrichment or extra-credit activities.

Try to anticipate problems students may encounter in the lesson or assignments. Check for new terms and be ready to define them and present examples. Do some of the classwork or homework assignment yourself to uncover hurdles students will face. You can then build some helpful hints into your lesson or give extra emphasis to these difficult areas.

Presenting new content.   If students understand where a lesson is going, they are more likely to be there with you at the end. Tell students what the lesson objectives are, either at the beginning of the activity or during it. If the lesson is at all complex, give students an outline to help them follow its organization. An outline helps organize the content for the students and provides a road map to keep them on course.

As you present a lesson, stay with the planned sequence unless an obvious change is needed. Avoid needless digressions, interruptions, or tangential information. Inserting irrelevant information into a lesson only confuses students about what they are expected to learn. Displaying key concepts, new terms, major points, and other critical information on the overhead transparency screen or the chalkboard will underscore their importance.

Presentations should be as focused and concrete as possible. Use examples, illustrations, demonstrations, physical props, charts, and any other means of providing substance and dimension to abstractions in the lesson. Avoid the vague expressions and verbal time fillers that, at best, communicate little information and always make presentations difficult to follow.

Checking for understanding.   Find out whether students understand a presentation *during* the lesson; do not wait until the next day.

As content development activities unfold, ask students questions to verify their comprehension of main points. You can also ask students to provide a written response to key questions and then check some or all of the students either orally or by examining the written work. Asking students to demonstrate comprehension at several points during a presentation not only allows you to verify their progress, but it keeps students more involved in the lesson.

You can also check student understanding and emphasize main points by conducting an oral recitation after a presentation. Do this by asking a series of questions that recapitulate the lesson sequence and its major concepts. Be sure to involve many students in answering these questions, so that you can identify the overall level of understanding in the class and reteach what has not been satisfactorily learned.

SUGGESTED ACTIVITIES

The two paragraphs below describe problems two teachers are experiencing with the management of instruction. After reading each paragraph, review Chapter Seven and decide what strategies they might use to help overcome the problem (other chapters may also provide useful suggestions). You might use each case as a basis for a group discussion and generate a list of many possible solutions or strategies. Then compare your list with the key in Appendix B.

Problem 7–1

During reading instruction Mr. Hart generally works with a small group of students while the remaining students do assigned work. Lately Mr. Hart has noticed that some students are not following seatwork directions and never finish their work, although he feels he allows appropriate amounts of time for work to be completed and gives thorough instructions before the reading groups start. A few students finish early, turn in their papers, and then wander around, interrupting other students and socializing excessively. Mr. Hart has to stop his work with the group in order to quiet the students down. What can Mr. Hart do to get students to work more productively during seatwork?

Problem 7–2

Ms. Jones is very frustrated because her students do not seem to listen to instruction. She explains carefully what to do, writes the assignment on the board, and asks for student questions. Nevertheless, before the class really gets started on the work, three or four students typically come up to the teacher's desk with questions. Others turn to their neighbors with questions. After answering the same questions for several students, she has to interrupt everyone to go back over instructions. Or, she later finds that some students have done their work incorrectly. What can this teacher do to help her students listen to and understand her instructions?

CHAPTER EIGHT
MANAGING
SPECIAL
GROUPS

Although the classroom management principles and guidelines discussed in previous chapters of this book apply to most classroom settings, classroom management is also affected by the characteristics of students making up the class. The ages, academic ability levels, goals, interests, and home backgrounds of students have an impact on their classroom behavior. Consequently, adjustments in management and instructional organization practices are sometimes needed to meet the needs of different groups of students. Two groups that frequently present some special challenges are classes that have significant numbers of students who are workng below grade level in basic skills and classes that are very heterogeneous. A heterogeneous class is one with significant differences in entering achievement levels of students. (Heterogeneity can also refer to other characteristics of students, but in this chapter it will be used mainly to refer to a range of student achievement or academic ability.) For example, a very heterogeneous fourth-grade class might include some students reading at first-grade levels or below, others reading at or near grade level, and some reading well above fourth-grade level. Meeting the needs of such a diverse group of students requires special effort. This chapter presents some information and suggestions that, combined with the principles described in previous chapters, will help you organize and manage heterogeneous classes and low-ability classes successfully. Because all classes are to some extent heterogeneous and most classes include some low-achieving students, many of the strategies suggested in this chapter will be helpful in any class.

ASSESSING ENTERING ACHIEVEMENT

In order to determine the degree of heterogeneity in your classroom or to identify low-achieving students, you should use several sources of information. These sources include tests you administer, your own observation of each child, and indicators of performance available in each child's file, including assessments obtained from prior teachers and standardized achievement test information. Of course, you should be cautious about forming a hasty impression of a child's abilities based on only one source of information. Furthermore, you must guard against the possibility of a negative self-fulfilling prophecy—allowing low expectations to be communicated to students, causing them to achieve below their potential.

Because of the importance of reading, language arts, and mathematics skills in the elementary school curriculum, these subjects will be the major focus of your initial assessment. As you evaluate your students, you should also be alert to indicators of study and work habits, such as the ability to follow directions and to maintain attention to a task. Children with very poor work skills or who are highly distractable may require special consideration in your room arrangement, in planning for instructional activities, and in monitoring.

When obtaining information about entering reading and math skill levels, special attention must be given to those students for whom you lack data. Typically, these will be students who have transferred from another school district. You must also be careful about the assessment of children for whom existing information is not consistent. It is especially important to assess such children individually by listening to them read and checking their vocabulary and word attack skills and by testing to identify their math skills. You should consult with other teachers and/or other professionals for help in selecting suitable assessment procedures if you do not already have them.

It is best to delay individual student assessment until several days after the beginning of school. During such testing it will be difficult for you to monitor your class, and you may also have to leave students too long in seatwork. By delaying testing, you will have a chance to observe the students, and the students will become better acquainted and more comfortable with you before they are tested. If you do individual testing, plan enough work to keep your class busy. When several students need to be assessed, space the testing over several days.

IDENTIFYING SPECIAL GROUPS

For the purpose of classroom instruction, the most important considerations are the range of entering achievement in basic skill subjects and the degree to which individual students are unable to work effectively with the grade-level curriculum. Of course, other characteristics of children can also affect learning and instruction—student interests and backgrounds, for example—and these should be considered whenever possible as you plan instructional activities and set goals. Especially in the basic skills, wide ranges of entering achievement create special problems. Knowing what is meant by high heterogeneity may be helpful in deciding when extra measures need to be taken. Consider a fourth-grade classroom with high heterogeneity in arithmetic achievement at the beginning of the year. Such a class would have some students whose math skills were barely above first-grade level and others who had the computational and conceptual proficiency of the average fifth or sixth grader. Thus, the lowest level of students might still be working on basic addition and subtraction facts while the

"I'm an underachiever....
What's your racket?"

highest level students might have mastered whole-number multiplication and be fairly proficient in simple long division. The same relative ability range in reading might find some students who could read only first-grade material or preprimers with few errors while the more capable readers in the class would be able to read and comprehend material whose vocabulary was at a level several grades higher.

In addition to the range between the most and least able students, the number of students at different levels is also an important consideration. For example, one class might have only one or two students at very high or very low levels, yet another class might have more students working at the extremes.

Designing classroom activities and adapting the curriculum to accommodate such wide diversity is challenging, to say the least. Very low-achieving students who confront the grade-level curriculum with no extra assistance will quickly encounter failure and frustration. Very high-achieving students may be bored and will not progress at a rate commensurate with their abilities if they are not provided with challenging learning tasks. It may be tempting to conclude that the key to coping with extreme diversity or with very low-achieving students is to individualize learning activities so that each student's special abilities and needs can be met. While an individualized program may in fact be beneficial for some students in some subject areas, such an approach is no panacea. In fact, it has a number of pitfalls—more materials to prepare, diversion of teacher time from instruction to evaluation and record keeping, and more difficulty with monitoring, to name three important problems. Consequently, many effective teachers deal with extreme heterogeneity and low-achieving students mainly by adapting an existing instructional program and associated activities. Only when simple adaptations are not adequate should more complex measures be used. This makes sense because many common features of the elementary school setting (such as the use of groups for basic skills instruction and resource room assignment for children with special needs) already address the problem of accommodating diversity.

STRATEGIES FOR INDIVIDUAL DIFFERENCES

In the next sections we will describe some strategies frequently used to adjust for individual differences and examine management concerns associated with these.

Team Teaching

Teachers at the same grade level frequently form teams to deal with heterogeneous student populations. Some students can then be reassigned to different teachers on the team for instruction in one or more subjects. This allows teachers to form relatively more homogeneous subgroups than would be possible using only students initially assigned to their individual classrooms. For example, two or three students whose entering reading skills are extremely low might be grouped for reading instruction with similar students from other classrooms. At the same time students at the highest level in the classes might be combined into a single group and taught by another teacher on the team. This arrangement permits instruction for these students to be targeted closer to their skill levels than if the students remained in their original classes.

Team approaches to student heterogeneity can be applied to a variety of subjects but are most common in reading and mathematics instruction. Teaming should be considered whenever the range of student ability is too great to be accommodated by three groups in reading and by two groups in mathematics. Although extreme heterogeneity within a class could theoretically be accommodated by forming more groups, to do so is usually not practical because it would place excessive demands on teacher planning and would reduce the amount of time each group receives for instruction. Because teaming requires careful planning and cooperation, the following items are important to consider.

Coordination of schedules.   The teachers on the team must establish compatible schedules for the subjects being team taught. If teachers deviate from the schedule without warning children from other classrooms may be kept waiting with nothing to do, and everyone will be thrown off schedule.

Student movement.   Because some students will be going from one room to another, expectations for behavior during these transitions must be communicated to the students. A teacher should accompany children in transit between rooms, at least until they have learned the routine.

Reminding students what they are supposed to take with them.   Sometimes children have trouble remembering their materials. When they do not bring the appropriate materials, they may be sent back to their classrooms, losing valuable instructional time and sometimes disturbing students in both rooms. If students will need different sets of materials on different days, all teachers involved should be notified so they can help students remember what will be needed when, perhaps by posting a list of materials to take or by reminding students as they prepare to leave the room.

Rules and procedures.   Students coming to you from another teacher's class will not know your expectations for their behavior. Therefore you will need to discuss rules for conduct and the procedures needed for small-group work and seatwork. Do this when you first meet with your new students. Then monitor them carefully until good behavior becomes established. If possible, plan rules and procedures with other members of the team in order to establish a common set of expectations. Consistency across settings will simplify the task of teaching students to behave correctly.

Maintaining responsibility for work.   In addition to rules for conduct and procedures for behavior, care must be taken to keep students responsible for their work. This may be harder to do in a team-teaching situation than with the students in your regular class because the full range of incentives, penalties, and parental contact may be limited. Also, you will not be able to supervise the students at other times of the day when they might have an opportunity to work on assignments (and when, ideally, you would check work and provide supplementary instruction). For these reasons, several steps should be followed to keep students accountable.

> Be certain that students, especially younger children, realize that you are responsible for checking their work and assigning a report card grade.
>
> Be clear about your expectations for work, other requirements, and your grading criteria.
>
> When you meet with students each day, check their work before you dismiss them, and give students whatever feedback they will need to complete the work successfully.
>
> Return graded papers promptly. Don't let these materials accumulate.
>
> Contact parents if children begin to skip assignments in your class. Don't rely on the homeroom teacher to do this.

Modifying Whole-Class Instruction

In some subjects the use of small groups for instruction will not be feasible or even desirable. Limited time, the problem of ascertaining individual differences on relevant entering skills, and greater procedural complexity may make small-group instruction less efficient than whole-class instruction. When used for subjects such as science or social studies, whole-class instruction can be modified to accommodate extremes in student abilities and interests. A number of simple modifications and cautions should be considered.

Interactive instruction.   You should try to involve *all* the students in presentations, discussions, and recitations. Do so by making a conscious effort to call on all students, not just those who are eager to respond. Students with a special ability or an obvious interest in a topic can be encouraged to complete special projects and to organize their ideas in oral reports to the class. These opportunities will allow the students to advance their understanding and receive recognition.

Seating arrangements.   Students who need closer supervision or more than the usual amount of explanation should be seated near the front of the room (or wherever you usually conduct whole-class presentations). Their proximity to you will enable you to check for understanding more readily and make it easier to monitor their behavior and progress.

Directions.   Communicating instructions and directions to a highly diverse class requires care. Be certain you have all students' attention and provide both oral and written directions when feasible. The use of questions to verify comprehension and careful monitoring will also be helpful. Be certain to check with those students who frequently have problems following directions. If you have seated them near you, then you will be able to provide them with added assistance as needed.

Assignments.   If you give the same assignments to all the students in a highly heterogeneous class, the work may be much too easy for some students and much too difficult for others. Consider giving assignments in two parts: a basic assignment for all students to complete and a second more difficult part that is assigned to some students or that can be completed for extra credit. When assignments are the same for everyone, the students will complete them with different degrees of proficiency and speed. In such cases, use a grading or credit system that, at least in part, emphasizes individual student progress rather than competition among students. Enrichment or extra-credit material for students who finish classwork early should be work-related and should not distract other students. Avoid free-time activities that are so attractive that slower-working students feel deprived or attempt to quit or rush through their work. Set up a system for giving credit, feedback, or recognition for completion of enrichment activities. If you allow students to read when they finish work, be sure to provide supplementary reading materials at a variety of reading levels.

Supplementary (Pull-out) Instruction

Sometimes students' needs in some subject areas cannot be well met in a regular classroom. For example a child's skills may be so deficient in reading or math that he or she cannot profit from small-group instruction; even the lowest group may be too far beyond the child's current level. Or a child may be so distracted by the stimulation of twenty-five or thirty students in a regular classroom that he or she cannot focus on assignments long enough to complete them. Such children may fall behind in their performance, even though they possess average or above-average ability. Children whose first language is not English may need intensive help that cannot be provided in the regular instructional program. Finally, some children may possess special talents that programs for the gifted can more fully develop. In all of these cases supplementary programs may be available. The term *pull-out* is sometimes applied to these programs because the children are taken out of the regular classroom for part of the school day in order to receive special instruction. Examples of pull-out programs include the following.

> Special education: Usually available in a "resource" room. Children with learning disabilities and other conditions that interfere with learning or adjustment in a regular classroom setting receive instruction (usually reading and/or math) for part of the day. These children return to the regular classroom for other instruction.
>
> Chapter I programs: These are special programs established in schools that serve children from lower-income families. Students with deficits in academic skills receive supplementary instruction from special teachers.
>
> Enrichment programs: Programs that provide enrichment in particular subjects are often established for students who have special talent in the area. These programs frequently use community resources, parents, or other volunteers as well as the regular teaching staff to provide programs during school hours or after hours.

The aspect of supplementary programs that has a major impact on your classroom management plan will be the removal of students from your classroom during the time that regular instruction is proceeding. Thus, scheduling must be carefully planned so that the pull-out students do not miss essential instruction and so that the other students' instructional program is not interrupted. Transitions out of and back into your classroom can become a major headache if they are not handled well.

Coordinating times with other teachers.   As soon as schoolwide schedules are set for lunch periods and activities such as music, art, and physical education classes, plan a schedule with the other teachers that will be as convenient as possible for everyone. If a number of students leave for special reading instruction, try to arrange with the reading teacher to have these students leave in a group at a time when you will be meeting with a reading group in your class. If several students will be pulled out for special instruction in a subject such as mathematics, you will probably want to schedule your math instruction for the rest of the class at that time.

Staying on schedule.   When class schedules involve pull-outs and drop-ins, it is especially important for teachers to stay on schedule so that students can be where they need to be at appropriate times. Have a large clock placed where everyone can see it. If you have trouble remembering to look at the clock, enlist the aid of the students in prompting you. Older students should eventually assume responsibility for their own schedules. You may want to post a list of times when different students are supposed to leave, in order to remind both you and the students. You can also set a timer as a reminder.

Having something for drop-in students to do while waiting for instruction.   Sometimes a teacher is not quite through with one group when it is time for another group to meet. Students who are working at their desks in the teacher's room should have enough activities to keep them busy. However, drop-in students sometimes arrive early and have nowhere specific to sit, other than in the small group. You will need a procedure for dealing with these students so that small groups and seatworkers are not distracted. Some teachers tell students to take an empty seat while waiting. Other teachers set aside a "waiting area" on a small rug or at a table. While there, students can get a copy of their textbook or workbook and begin reading the next lesson or do other constructive activities.

Getting returning students involved again.   After receiving instruction outside the room, some pull-out students may tend to dawdle or seem confused about what they are supposed to do when they return to the room. The best way to avoid confusion is to establish routines so that students always know what to do when they return. It is a good idea to post assignments or give students a list of assignments to help them remember. At the beginning of the school year make a special effort to establish a routine. If, for example, you are working with a small group when some students return, give the small group something to do and go to the returning students to be sure they get back on task. Student helpers could also be given the responsibility for explaining the assignment or activity to individual returning students.

Activities when supplementary instruction is not held.   Sometimes the special teacher will be absent or the special class will not be conducted for some other reason. When this occurs it is important to have something for these students to do while you carry on with regular instruction. In some cases students may be included in regular class activities. In other cases you will have to provide special activities. If possible, meet regularly with the other teachers so that you will know what students are working on and be able to assign appropriate tasks. Try to have some free-time or enrichment activities set aside to accommodate varying levels of ability. It is important to monitor these students and give them something meaningful to do; otherwise, they may become bored or disruptive.

In-class aides.   Sometimes teachers are fortunate enough to have parents or other adult volunteers, teacher aides, or university education students to help out in their classrooms. These aides may be assigned to help with a particular subject or be available to help with any subject. Other aides may help with materials and administrative tasks and have little contact with the children. If you have one or more aides, there are several things you will need to do to promote smooth functioning in your classroom. You should inform the aide of his or her responsibilities for teaching or working with students and for disciplining students. All aides should be aware of your classroom rules and procedures. You will probably want aides to enforce your rules consistently when they are in charge of students. If you must leave the room, inform students that the aide will be in charge of the class and will enforce the rules as you do. If the aide will be working with individual students or small groups, you will need to make available a space that will not cause distractions for the rest of the class, particularly if you are instructing simultaneously. Students should be told whether and when they may go to the aide for help.

Individualized Instruction

When each student receives instruction and is given assignments at a level established by careful assessment of the student's entering skills and is encouraged to progress at whatever pace his or her abilities and motivation allow, then the instructional program is said to be individualized. Some educators consider individualized instruction to be the best means of coping with heterogeneity because it offers, at least in principle, instruction tailored to the needs of each child. However, individualized instruction is difficult to implement. It requires (1) careful and continuous assessment of individual pupil progress, (2) management of time so that all students receive adequate interactive instruction from the teacher, (3) sufficient resources, including materials suitable for all ability levels in the class, and (4) the time for the teacher to plan and develop appropriate activities. The absence of one or more of these features will make it difficult to mount an effective instructional program. Also, teachers who wish to implement such programs should do so gradually, allowing themselves adequate time to develop the necessary resources. Because of these difficulties, we regard the first lines of defense for coping with heterogeneity and low-achieving students to be the modification of whole-class instruction, supplementary instruction, and team teaching. Only when these strategies are not adequate should individualized instruction be necessary.

When individualization of instruction is used for one or more subjects, you should anticipate a number of management problems and take action to prevent them or at least minimize their impact.

Transitions. Students engaged in individual rather than group activities will generally end their activities at different times. If the next activity is also an individual activity, then many individual transitions will occur throughout the period of instruction. This can cause much confusion and lost time. Some students may not know what to do; others may delay starting the next activity. More efficient transitions can be effected if the teacher is alert to help students who are between activities. Assignments must be posted or written somewhere so that students will know what to do next. The teacher can also have students bring completed work to be checked in order to provide some structure during the transition and to be certain that students know how to get started on the next activity.

Student movement. Movement between locations of activities is more difficult to manage when students complete or start activities at varying times. Because the teacher is frequently working with one or a few students at a time, less supervision of movement is possible, and students may begin to wander around frequently, wasting time and distracting other students. Student movement should be regulated by procedures that make clear when and for what purpose students may move around, converse with other students, or be out of their seats. Identifying the reason for excessive wandering or out-of-seat behavior can be helpful in remedying it. If students have completed their work satisfactorily and have nothing to do, then more challenging work or enrichment is appropriate. If students quit working because they are not able to do the assignment, then additional instruction, assistance, or modified assignments are in order.

Monitoring student behavior. Different expectations for students in different activities along with a variety of simultaneous activities make monitoring student behavior during individualized instruction difficult. Also, the teacher often instructs individual students or performs other tasks associated with individualized instruction (such as assessment), thus adding to the complexity of monitoring. To overcome these problems, the following key behaviors should be practiced.

Know what all students are supposed to be doing at any given time so that you can support their efforts and prevent problems.

Be sure students know what they are expected to do and what conduct is appropriate in different activities.

Be alert for students who are having difficulty getting started or completing an activity so that you can provide help. Don't get overly engrossed with helping one or a few students, and don't wait until students quit working or become disruptive before providing assistance. Circulate among the students and look at their work periodically. Scan the room frequently to detect early signs of frustration or task avoidance.

Usually a few students will require more supervision than others. When possible, be sure these students are seated where you can observe and assist them readily.

Encouraging student responsibility for work.   The use of an individualized instruction program does not guarantee that students will accept responsibility for completing assignments and participating in learning activities. In fact, some students will take advantage of the more complex instructional arrangements and limitations on the teacher's monitoring capability to avoid responsibility and to expend minimal effort. To avoid these problems, you must give clear directions for assignments and other activities. Many teachers prefer to review directions with students at the beginning of the period devoted to the individualized instructional activities. A basic set of activities can often be listed on the chalkboard and reviewed, or students can be given activity or assignment folders that list what is to be done. Such a folder can also be used to check off completed work. This system helps both the teacher and the students keep track of progress. Setting time limits for work on one activity before proceeding to the next will help students pace their efforts.

Students should expect their work to be checked frequently. If they get accustomed to simply completing one activity and starting a new one without feedback, their performance will deteriorate. The teacher should develop monitoring procedures that include periodic progress checks and evaluation and feedback of completed assignments and other work. It is also important to review overall student progress and decide whether the pace and scope of work is adequate. Some teachers prefer weekly or biweekly reviews and a short conference with individual students for this purpose.

Sometimes the teacher's role in individualization diminishes to the point where almost all of the teacher's time is devoted to assessment, giving assignments, keeping records, and checking. When this occurs, students receive little interactive instruction from the teacher and do little except complete worksheets. The teacher's diminished instructional role may be partly due to the incorrect perception that because instruction is individualized, the teacher can only instruct one student at a time. In fact, it is far more efficient if the teacher presents information and conducts recitations with groups of students, supplementing these group lessons with individual instruction for students who require extra help.

Contracts.   These are often used with individual instruction. Contracts usually include a list of assignments or activities to be completed by a student during a fixed period of time, such as a day or a week. Contracts also may specify the goals or objectives, materials, and incentives associated with completing the contract. Use of a contract has a number of advantages. It is a good way to communicate assignments and objectives, it enables students to suggest modifications that they would find helpful or interesting, and the student's signature on the contract can increase motivation for completion within the agreed-upon time period.

Help from peers.   Another method for coping with extreme heterogeneity and for dealing with low achievers is to use students to help other students. Examples of such peer helping arrangements include the following.

> Students work in pairs, reading and listening to each other read. "Reading with a buddy" can be part of contract work.
>
> Certain students are assigned as monitors to help other students when the teacher is busy with group or individual instruction.
>
> When the teacher is busy with small-group instruction, students who need help are encouraged to get assistance from any other student before interrupting the teacher.
>
> Group leaders are assigned to each learning station to answer questions and to set up materials.
>
> A capable, mature student is assigned as a helper for another student who needs frequent assistance. The helper's responsibilities are to answer questions and explain directions.
>
> Students may be permitted to help or seek help from a neighbor on some seatwork activities.

When using students as helpers, you should recognize the potential for excessive noise, poor attention to the task, or excessive reliance on the helper by the helpee. Also, not all students are amenable to this type of arrangement or work well together. These negative effects can be averted by communicating clearly what is and is not permitted and by monitoring the helping arrangements and relationships to be sure no undesirable side effects develop. As is true for all of the variations from regular instructional patterns, gradual introduction of new arrangements will give the best opportunity for managing their implementation and for correcting problems.

TEACHING LOW-ACHIEVING STUDENTS

Many teachers feel they need help in organizing instruction to successfully teach students who are on a low academic level. Whether you have a class with only a few "low achievers" or one with many children whose entering skills are far below grade level, you will need to give some special attention to the instructional needs of these students.

In many cases students who are achieving substantially below grade level come from disadvantaged or low socioeconomic status (SES) backgrounds. Research has shown that these students may not benefit from the same teaching strategies that work with average or high-achieving students who have "learned how to learn" early in life. In addition, some techniques that are good instructional practices with all student populations are especially important when teaching low-achieving students.

Active Instruction

Research has shown that students at a low academic level make more progress in basic skills when their teachers provide structured classroom activities with close teacher supervision and lots of active, teacher-led instruction. Large amounts of class time spent in unstructured or free-time activities should be avoided, as should situations calling for frequent student self-direction and self-pacing. It is especially important for lower-achieving students to have many opportunities to interact with the teacher during instruction, and to answer teacher questions and receive feedback about their work. Lower-achieving students should be seated where they can be easily monitored and given assistance.

Organizing and Pacing Instruction

When teaching lower-achieving students, you can encourage more student learning and better classroom behavior if you break instruction into small segments or short activities with frequent assessments of student understanding. Avoid activity plans that require students to attend to a presentation or to work for twenty-five or thirty minutes at a stretch in the same seatwork assignment. Instead, use two or more shorter cycles of content development and work samples in each lesson, as described in Chapter Seven. There are two distinct advantages of using several cycles instead of one when teaching lower ability students. One advantage is that it is easier to maintain student involvement over shorter times. Also, by carefully monitoring, you can easily observe whether students are able to complete the assignments, which in turn makes it easier for you to pace instruction appropriately and give ample feedback to students.

In planning lessons, keep in mind that especially with lower-ability students it is better to cover material very thoroughly than to cover a lot of material quickly. Plan for plenty of practice and repetition, and keep your lesson plans flexible enough to allow for reteaching. Plan introductions of new content very carefully. Clear communication is important in all classes, but it is especially important when teaching lower-achieving students. Careless, overly complex communication is likely to result in student confusion, frustration, and misbehavior. Follow the guidelines for clarity discussed in Chapter Seven, paying careful attention to the amount of information presented at one time, appropriate vocabulary, and the use of concrete or specific examples to illustrate new concepts. Check for student understanding frequently. Avoid overlapping many procedural directions. Get students' attention, then present directions in a step-by-step fashion, waiting for students to complete each step before going on to the next.

Remedial Instruction

For learning to occur, all students (and especially lower-achieving students) must be provided with instructional materials and tasks at which they can succeed. Lower-achieving students often require remedial instruction. When beginning a new unit you may find that some students do not have prerequisite skills. Or after teaching a lesson you may realize that several students have not mastered the new skill. Both of these situations require that you provide remedial instruction. Two considerations are crucial: You must build time for remediation into your classroom activity plans, and you must get instructional materials that are appropriate for the students who need remediation. Talk with your instructional supervisor, a resource teacher, or other teachers to obtain instructional materials that your low-ability students will be able to complete successfully.

Building Positive Attitudes

Even in lower elementary grades, relatively low-achieving students are more likely to have developed a poor self-image or poor attitude toward school. By the upper elementary grades low-academic-level students have often fallen two or more grade levels below average for their grade and age group. Some may have failed one or more grades in previous years. Because of their frequent failure in school in the past, some of these students will have become very discouraged; they may react by giving up easily or by fighting back. These reactions may be evidenced in the extremes of apathy, shyness, belligerence, or clowning in class. Especially in earlier grades these students may perceive classroom events as arbitrary or mysterious. They do not expect to understand and be successful at classroom tasks. Maintaining their attention for long periods of time may be difficult, particularly when they encounter demanding or frustrating tasks. As a teacher of lower-achieving students, an important part of your task is to improve these students' self-images and expectations of accomplishment. There are several steps you can take. First, remember that it is important for these students to finish their work and not give up. This may require that you shorten assignments for some or provide students with extra time and encouragement to finish their work. Be careful, however, that the extra time low-achieving students are given to finish assignments does not prevent them from participating in interesting and worthwhile activities with the rest of the class. Being denied participation in show-and-tell, art activities, interest centers, and recess will not contribute to an improved self-image! A better approach is to provide materials and assignments that lower-achieving students are able to finish in the available time.

The way you treat lower-achieving students during class discussions can also make a difference in their attitude and achievement. During large-group or small-group lessons or discussion sessions, "stay with" students until they are able to answer a question. Don't let another student quickly answer the question given to a lower-achieving student, and don't accept a wrong answer from a low achiever, leaving the student with little or no feedback. Reword questions or help students give an acceptable answer.

A warm, supporting, and accepting classroom climate will benefit lower-achieving students, but be thoughtful in your use of praise. Research suggests that praise is more helpful when it is specific and contingent on good work and/or good behavior. Don't make the mistake of frequently "rewarding" low-achieving students with vague or general praise or praise for wrong answers or sloppy, incomplete work. This kind of teacher behavior may confuse students or convey the message that you don't expect much from them. Be alert for opportunities to give slower students deserved and specific praise.

SUGGESTED ACTIVITIES

1. Read Case Study 8–1 at the end of the chapter to see one teacher's strategies for working with students with low reading levels.

2. Problems 8–1 and 8–2 below describe two situations that elementary teachers frequently encounter. Use ideas presented in this chapter to identify some strategies that could be used in these situations.

Problem 8–1: Team Teaching

Mr. Miller and two other fourth-grade teachers use team teaching for math instruction. Shortly after lunch each day, some students from the other teachers' classes come to Mr. Miller's room, while some of his students go to the other two teachers' rooms. Mr. Miller has grown dissatisfied with the arrangement because he feels that too much of his teaching time is wasted while groups change rooms, get organized, and get ready to work. Sometimes early-arriving students disrupt lessons. At other times, stragglers hold up the rest of the class. Students frequently arrive without the materials they need for that day. While Mr. Miller answers questions and deals with problems, students begin chatting and wandering around. When Mr. Miller is ready to start the lesson, he has trouble getting students settled down to work. What can Mr. Miller do to make teaming work more smoothly?

Problem 8–2: A Heterogeneous Class

Ms. Ortiz feels that her class this year is more difficult to teach than any she has had in her four years of teaching third grade. Of twenty-six students in class, seven are beginning the school year functioning at first-grade level or below in reading. Five of these seven are also far behind in mathematics concepts; the other two are on grade level. Three students in the class have advanced reading and mathematics skills, while others are nearer to grade level. Ms. Ortiz is frustrated in her attempts to meet the needs of the slowest students while challenging the brighter students. She now conducts four reading groups. What strategies might Ms. Ortiz consider trying?

CASE STUDY 8–1: ORGANIZING READING GROUP ACTIVITIES FOR LOW-ACADEMIC-LEVEL STUDENTS

Ms. Barstow had a group of boys who were very low achievers in reading and who had great difficulty in keeping themselves on-task. Rather than giving them independent assignments, as she could do with some others in the class, she arranged their reading activities so that she could give them small chunks of instruction and frequent feedback. She met with their reading group first. During instruction, she asked many questions with relatively short answers, calling on each child in the group in turn. She avoided letting any one student talk at length or wander from the academic question at hand. In this way she was able to keep everyone's attention focused on the work.

After carefully going over directions and checking students' comprehension of them, the teacher dismissed the group to perform a specific assignment at the listening center, where her voice on the prepared tape provided continuous direction. Later she met with them again briefly to check their work and to give them another short assignment. They were given about twenty minutes to work independently, and the teacher sat so that she could monitor them while she taught another group. After doing their seatwork assignment, they went to a Language Master machine (as previously directed by the teacher) to practice skills while the teacher worked with another group. Then the teacher quickly checked over the first group's and other children's work and ended the morning's reading group activities. Because the teacher had selected activities and arranged the schedule so that these boys did not have to depend on their own self control for long periods of time, the boys were engaged in and attending to instructions or actively practicing skills for most of the morning.

CHAPTER NINE
EVALUATING
YOUR CLASSROOM'S
ORGANIZATION
AND MANAGEMENT

Effective teachers frequently stop to consider how well their classes are functioning, then they make changes to improve things when necessary. They are alert to whether class time is being used productively, whether students are making satisfactory progress, and whether the class environment is as pleasant and conducive to learning as it should be. If they identify an aspect that could be improved, they are systematic in identifying the source of the problem, seeking solutions, and making changes in their own behavior or their classroom's organization. For most teachers, however, evaluating and improving their classroom management and organization is not an easy undertaking, for several reasons. First, many teachers especially inexperienced ones, are unsure of what *criteria* to use in judging their classroom management or what levels of management success to expect. After all, no class of elementary students is completely cooperative and task-oriented, and no teacher is totally organized, efficient, and clear at all times. Furthermore, teachers seldom have the opportunity to observe other teachers' classrooms, so they may have a limited perspective from which to view their own situation. Finally, it is difficult for teachers both to teach and to observe their own classes systematically unless they have a very clear idea of what management indicators are important.

This chapter is designed to help you as you evaluate or make plans to improve your own management effectiveness. First, we shall identify some major indicators of management effectiveness and suggest levels of acceptable or "expectable" class performance for each. Next, to help you diagnose the causes of a problem, we have provided a series of questions relating to each of six areas that are often the basis for management problems. Because the areas and questions are keyed to the chapters in this book, this chapter will also serve as a basis for applying and reviewing key concepts and principles that have been emphasized. Problem vignettes presented at the end of the chapter will allow you to test your skills at diagnosing management difficulties and identifying alternate courses of action.

DETERMINING WHEN CHANGES ARE NEEDED

To decide whether or where there might be room for improvement in the management or organization of your classroom, we suggest that you consider the effects of your management system on the behavior of your students. Using student behavior as criteria for management effectiveness makes sense because one of the main goals of classroom management is to foster student cooperation and involvement in learning activities. Also, student behaviors provide management indicators that are relatively easy to observe. For example, major signs of management problems include frequent failure by many students to complete assignments satisfactorily, high rates of off-task behavior, widespread lack of cooperation, and frequent disruption of classroom activities. What constitutes acceptable or desirable levels of class behavior on each of these indicators? This is difficult to state with certainty because of differing school practices, tolerance levels of teachers and students, and varying expectations for behavior for different activities, groups of students, and age/grade levels. We will, however, provide approximate guidelines for levels of these indicators that are often seen in well-managed classrooms. These estimates are based on observations from our own research as well as on data from other studies using measures of student behavior.

On-task rates. This indicator is defined as the number of students who are appropriately engaged in whatever classroom activity is occurring. Being on-task does not necessarily mean that a student is highly involved or participating enthusiastically; it does mean that no obvious sign of inattention or inappropriate behavior is apparent and that the student is doing whatever the situation calls for. On-task rates vary somewhat across activities. In teacher-led whole-class activities, a well-managed class typically will have on-task rates of about 90 percent or higher. Thus in a class of twenty-five to thirty students, no more than two or three students on the average would be off-task at any given time in such activities. In seatwork not directly supervised by the teacher (for example, while the teacher is working with a small group) lower rates would usually be found among students doing seatwork. Off-task students would generally *not* be engaged in disruptive behavior, but they might be momentarily socializing, out of their seats, daydreaming, or simply not working. We would not usually expect any individual student to remain off-task for very long, certainly not throughout an entire activity.

Disruptive behavior.   Student behavior is disruptive when it seriously interferes with the activities of the teacher or several students for more than a brief time. Examples of such behavior include continuously bothering neighboring students, creating confusion or making loud noises during a lesson, excessive attention seeking, acting out, and running around the room, as well as hostile, aggressive responses to other students or to the teacher. Disruptive behavior varies in intensity from relatively mild forms to very severe types. In well-managed classes disruptive behaviors are not common and are usually limited to mild and brief incidents, generally occurring no more than once per hour. When a more severe disturbance occurs, it is almost always an isolated incident, and the teacher takes immediate action to deal with it.

Student cooperation.   Well-managed classrooms usually are pleasant environments for students and the teacher. Students should not, after the first several weeks of classes, need constant reminders to follow rules and procedures, and they should follow the teacher's directions without excessive delay or complaints. They should be tolerant of each other's needs and willing to abide by group decisions and work within the class routines that the teacher has established. A problem in this area is indicated when many students continue to test limits, disregard class rules and major procedures, and display rudeness and intolerance toward each other or the teacher.

Completion of assignments.   Although failure to complete assignments suggests instructional or learning difficulties, it can also be an indicator of management problems. When we speak of *frequent* failure to complete assignments, we mean that more than one or two students often do not complete their work on time. This may involve the same students or different students. Of course, any student who frequently fails to complete assignments should be of concern and given your attention. However, it is only when *several* students frequently fail to complete assignments that a management problem is suggested. Although classroom management variables are not likely to be the sole causes, changes in accountability procedures, rewards, or in the way instruction is organized and presented can help alleviate the problem.

If levels of on-task behavior, disruption, cooperation, and assignment completion in your classroom are very different from the levels in well-managed classes described in the preceding paragraphs, adjustments in your management system may be called for. Some allowances should be made, however, for student behavior in very early grades, in very large classes, and in classes with many low-achieving students or a high proportion of boys. Such classes will often have more off-task or inappropriate behavior (not that you will encourage it!). Thus you might have one or two more off-task students on the average, and perhaps a bit more frequent disruptive behavior before you should get concerned that management problems may be developing. Also, you should not overreact to an occasional bad day or lesson. It will often be more difficult to maintain student involvement on the day before a holiday and late Friday afternoon. The key question is this: Are one or more management indicators at undesirable levels on a regular basis? If so, then you should evaluate your management plan and try to improve it. Note that the presence of a problem does not mean that a class is poorly managed. Even teachers with good management skills can still have some room for improvement. Solving a particular management problem may change an average situation into an excellent one. However, even classrooms with widespread management problems can be improved. The time and effort required will eventually pay off with better student behavior and a classroom setting more conducive to learning.

You may wish to gather more evidence before proceeding. One way to gather more data is to keep a log of class behavior for a week. Write a short daily summary of the events and behavior that take place during activities that seem to have problems. This record will allow you to decide whether problems are recurrent and not just the result of unusual circumstances. The process of keeping a record may also help you identify what is *causing* the difficulties. Another possibility for gathering evidence is to ask a colleague to observe you teach. Although the opportunity to observe fellow teachers is limited, someone might be able to observe you when a subject specialist, such as a music teacher, is teaching his or her classes. Another possibility is to ask an administrator, supervisor, or a special teacher whose schedule may be more flexible to observe you. Needless to say, such a person must be one whose opinion you trust and who will be helpful rather than threatening to you. Before the observation, talk with your observer about the areas that concern you and about the kind of feedback you would like to receive.

DIAGNOSING THE CAUSES OF A PROBLEM

Once a problem is recognized, the next step is to identify its cause. Self-diagnosis is always an uncertain art, so if possible, you should seek the advice of others, preferably those who have observed you in your class. In addition, the following suggestions in six basic areas will help pinpoint sources of management problems. This self-evaluation guide is keyed to relevant chapters of this book. It is organized into six management areas, with specific indicators to help you identify sources of possible problems in each areas. Even if you are not experiencing management problems to any great degree, you may find it helpful to review the guide. You may discover an item or two that you could modify with good effect.

1. Reevaluate Your Room Arrangement

Ask yourself these questions to determine if your classroom space and materials are well organized:

> Does congestion frequently occur in certain areas of the room, such as at the pencil sharpener, materials center, small-group areas, or your desk?
>
> Can you and your students move around the room easily, or are traffic lanes blocked by desks, other furniture, or equipment?
>
> Do students at the small-group area or at centers distract nearby students from their seatwork?
>
> Can you see all students from any place in the room at which you instruct or work?
>
> During your presentations, can students see the overhead projector or screen and the main chalkboard areas without turning around or moving from their chairs or desks?
>
> Are students who frequently need your attention or assistance seated where you can easily monitor and reach them?
>
> Do some students frequently bother others who sit near them?

If you have answered yes to one or more of the above questions, then some aspects of your room arrangement could be at fault and a change may be in order. If the problem is obvious and easily corrected, such as a change of seats for a few students who are distracting each other, make the change without delay. If the problem is more complicated, then use the material presented in Chapter One as a guide for comprehensive review of your present room arrangement.

Note that some of the problems implied by the preceding questions could have other contributing causes. For example, if students are distracting each other, the problem might be caused by poor monitoring, inadequate consequences, or excessively long periods of seatwork rather than the seating arrangement. Thus, consider your ideas about the causes of a problem as hypotheses that may or may not explain all of the situation. Don't let an initial insight blind you to other possibilities.

2. Review Your Rules and Procedures for Student Conduct

Have you stopped enforcing one or more of your rules?

Are your major class procedures, such as those governing student talk, raising hands, movement around the room, use of equipment and supplies, being followed without constant prompting and reminders?

Are some student behaviors occurring that are clearly undesirable, but that are not covered under your current rules or procedures?

Do you find yourself giving the same directions repeatedly for some common procedure?

Are you spending as much time going over directions and procedures now as at the beginning of the year?

Affirmative answers to these questions indicate potential problems in some procedural area. You will find it worthwhile to review Checklist 2 and the descriptions of commonly used procedures in Chapter Two. If you decide to modify an existing rule or procedure or to install a new one, do so as carefully as if it were the beginning of the year. Explain the change or new procedure clearly, demonstrate it if necessary, watch students as they follow the new procedure, and give them corrective or supportive feedback as appropriate.

The fact that a rule or procedure is not working does not necessarily mean that it is inappropriate and should be changed. It may mean that the procedure or rule needs better consequences or more careful monitoring. Thus before you change a major procedure, be sure to consider whether other aspects of your management system need a tune-up. In particular, you should review the material in Chapter Four on Rewards and Penalties.

3. Review Your Major Accountability Procedures

Do many of your students fail to complete assignments or not turn them in at all?

Is much student work messy to the point of being illegible?

Are students completing work on time, or do you find yourself giving extensions more and more frequently?

Do students sometimes claim that they didn't know an assignment was due or what its requirements were?

After grades are given on report cards, do students frequently complain that they do not understand why they received particular grades?

These questions indicate potential problems with accountability procedures, including grading, and with procedures for giving feedback, monitoring student work in progress, and communicating assignments and work requirements. Of course, other reasons for failure to complete assignments should be considered, including a mismatch between task demands and student capability or incomplete understanding of the content. However, a review of material in Chapter Three should provide some additional help in establishing better levels of student responsibility for their work.

4. List the Consequences for Appropriate and Inappropriate Behavior, and Review How Frequently They Are Used and How Effective They Are

Do you reward good student behavior, including effort, in a variety of ways?

Are your rewards still attractive to students, or have they tired of them?

Do you find yourself assessing penalties more and more often and rewarding students less than you previously did?

Are you warning and threatening students frequently, and do you fail to follow through when students continue to misbehave?

Have your penalties lost their deterrent value through overuse?

Does administering your reward or penalty system take too much time and effort?

You should consider occasionally varying or adding to your rewards, especially if they seem to be losing their appeal. Also, limited but consistent use of penalties is necessary in order for them to retain their effectiveness. Review the recommendations in Chapter Four for some ideas and examples of consequence systems. Also check Chapter Six for some simple strategies for dealing with inappropriate behavior without the use of penalties.

5. Consider Whether You Are Detecting Misbehavior in its Early Stages and Preventing Little Problems from Developing into Big Ones

Do you tend to notice misbehavior only after it involves several students?

When you work with students in groups or individually at your desk, does noise, disruption, or widespread work avoidance occur?

Do you sometimes have the feeling that some students are misbehaving simply to gain your attention?

Are there times when so much inappropriate behavior occurs at once that you don't have any idea what to do?

Do you sometimes discover that students have hardly begun classwork assignments when they should actually be through with them?

If you are experiencing problems in this area, you need to work on your skills for monitoring and dealing promptly with inappropriate behavior. Sometimes teachers who have difficulty catching misbehavior early tend to become overly absorbed in their immediate situation and lose sight (literally) of the whole classroom setting. Such tunnel vision causes them to overlook incipient problems at the periphery of the class. Small problems are likely to become big ones when teachers ignore too much inappropriate behavior, when they fail to use simple, unobtrusive strategies to help students get back on task, or when they overreact to relatively minor events, giving them inappropriate attention. Suggestions for monitoring and responding to inappropriate behavior can be found in Chapter Six.

6. Consider Ways to Improve the Management of Your Instructional Activities

Do students frequently seem confused about work requirements, and do they fail to follow directions, even after you have explained them or listed them on the board?

Do you often discover that students have not understood your presentations and that they therefore cannot complete assignments correctly?

When students are frequently confused and unable to follow directions, you should suspect problems with the clarity of presentations. Being clear involves more than just repeating information or instructions, so give careful consideration to the tips on teaching clearly in Chapter Seven.

Are transitions from one activity to another taking a long time?

Are some students not ready for instruction when a new activity begins?

Is there widespread misbehavior during transitions?

Transition points occur frequently over the course of a school day and can be a source of distress if they are not handled carefully. Ideas for structuring transitions are presented in Chapter Seven, along with the material on activity management and clarity.

Do you have students with learning problems who seem to require more assistance than you are giving them?

Is there a constant demand for free-time materials and activities in your class?

Is the performance of many of your students well below grade level in basic skills areas?

Are some of your students so fast at finishing classwork that they get bored or bother others?

Do you find that a relatively small group of students monopolizes class discussions?

Are a few of your students so far behind the class that you have just given up on them?

Ideas for managing classes with students working well below grade level or with a very wide ability range are presented in Chapter Eight. Good management in such classes is especially important because of the need to provide extra assistance and supervision for certain students.

IMPLEMENTING CHANGES IN YOUR CLASSROOM

If you decide that some change in your classroom management system is required, then you'll need to plan when and how to do it. Some changes will be simple to plan and carry out; others will be more complex.

Less complex changes.   The least complicated changes are those that involve only your own behavior. For example, you may decide that you need to review or reteach certain procedures, be more consistent in your enforcement of certain rules, or monitor student behavior and work more carefully. Such changes can be undertaken at once and require only your own resolve and self-monitoring to carry them out. However, succeeding in such a change may not be as easy as attempting it. Like New Year's resolutions, attempts to alter established behavior patterns are sometimes short-lived. Help yourself make such changes by *writing* down a plan that specifies exactly what you intend to do. For example, if you decide you are going to try to work on monitoring student behavior more carefully, you might make the following notes:

During whole-class presentations I will observe the class, looking at each student, at least twice a minute.

During seatwork I will check each student's progress during the first few minutes of the activity and at least one other time, and I will check the work of students who have problems completing assignments several other times.

During reading groups I will look around the room at least once every minute while I'm with a small group, and I will walk around the room to check student progress in between working with each group.

At the beginning of each day, read over your plan. Try to follow it consistently during class. Then review the plan at the end of each day to evaluate your progress and to make necessary alterations or additions. Besides committing yourself to a change, writing the plan out in detail will help make it more specific and concrete and therefore more likely to be implemented. If you find that you forget to carry out the plan, write notes to yourself, then put them in places that will remind you at appropriate times. For example, make notes on three by five cards—"Remember to monitor"—and clip one to your lesson plan book and others to the teacher's edition of one or two of your textbooks.

Other, less complicated changes are alterations in seating assignments, room arrangement, the schedule of activities, and procedures to regulate student behaviors that occur infrequently. For such changes, you might simply define the expected behavior or change, describe or discuss a rationale with the students, then monitor student compliance.

More complex changes.   Any change that requires students to alter frequently occurring behavior will be more complex than a change that involves only the teacher or a minor change by students. Not only are old habits hard to break but because the behavior occurs frequently, more opportunities will exist for students to avoid the new behaviors. An example of a more complex change is requiring students to raise their hands and wait to be called on after they have become accustomed to calling out without raising hands. Another more complex and difficult change is obtaining completed work from students who have become habitual work avoiders.

To bring about complex changes, several steps are necessary. The desired change and reasons for it should first be discussed with the students. During the discussion you should obtain a commitment from the students to make the change. You should also identify any new consequences for appropriate or inappropriate behavior. Then, once you have given the instructions, you must monitor initial trials carefully, provide corrective feedback, encouragement and rewards, as needed, and remain alert to proper implementation until the new behavior has taken hold.

When should changes be made?   Simple changes can be made at almost any time. They should not, however, be capricious. Before making a simple change (such as a change in room arrangement, grading procedures, procedures regulating infrequent student behavior), review other related aspects of your management system to be sure that you are altering the correct component. Then make the change whenever it appears appropriate.

More complex changes require careful planning. The greatest danger is that you might try change before you are ready for it. Once you have diagnosed a problem it will be natural to want to take immediate corrective action. However, if the change is not properly planned, it is less likely to succeed. Therefore, be sure to make major changes only after you have carefully considered alternatives. Be sure you know exactly what behaviors will be expected of students and that you have enough time to explain and to monitor the change. Once your planning is complete, you are ready to initiate the new behavior.

Good times to review your management plans and to make changes, especially major ones, are the start of a new grading period or the day immediately after a vacation break. Classes are usually more attentive and cooperative at such times, and they will be more accepting of change. Younger students are especially inclined to be forgetful and may need a review of class rules and procedures anyhow, which makes this a natural time to introduce a change. In fact, you can enlist the students' help in making changes by noting that they are starting a new grading period or beginning over after a vacation and that this is a chance to make a fresh start.

SUGGESTED ACTIVITIES

Three case studies of classes with management problems are presented below. After reading each one, try to identify the major problem areas and then describe what each teacher could do to manage these classes more effectively. After you have completed each case study, compare your suggestions to the answer key in the appendix. These case studies also provide good material for small-group discussions, because individuals will bring different perspectives to each case and different solutions may be offered.

CASE STUDY 9–1: MISBEHAVIOR IN A THIRD-GRADE CLASS

Ms. Wade's third-grade students never seem to settle down for very long. Regardless of whether the children have been assigned seatwork or are supposed to be paying attention to a presentation, some degree of commotion or noise is always present. During the first few days of school the class seemed well behaved and was seldom out of order, and almost all the children were cooperative and did their work. Gradually, however, more and more inappropriate socializing, loud talk, call-outs, and other interruptions occurred, even from previously quiet students.

During Ms. Wade's presentations to the class, students are frequently inattentive and she is able to complete lessons only with difficulty. Sometimes she even stops lessons short because the children are so difficult to control. At times the only way she can restore a semblance of quiet is to start writing names on the board and assigning detention. However, even that tactic doesn't work for very long, because so many students are inattentive that the list of names gets very long and not being on the list becomes something of a social stigma.

During a recent reading-group period, three students talked continuously while Ms. Wade was working with one of the small groups. Two other children wandered around the room and a half dozen others made frequent trips to the drinking fountain, rest rooms, and hamster cages.

What has gone wrong in this class? How might Ms. Wade attempt to produce better behavior?

CASE STUDY 9-2: POOR WORK AND STUDY HABITS IN A FIFTH-GRADE CLASS

Mr. Ambrose's fifth-grade class has been fairly well behaved and exhibits little disruptive behavior. Most students follow his procedures for procedural tasks such as staying in their seats during whole-class presentations, raising hands during discussions, and using the pencil sharpener, rest room, and other areas of the room appropriately. Some social talk occurs during seatwork activities, but it does not escalate into chaos and students usually settle down when requested. However, students have been less task-oriented lately and many students have been tardy turning in assignments. They complain that they don't know when assignments are due, and some don't turn in their work at all. In order to make assignments very explicit, Mr. Ambrose has begun to record the daily assignments on the side chalkboard. Because some assignments are not due until the following day, he leaves the previous day's assignments on that chalkboard also, so students will know when each subject's assignment is due for both days.

Today during a one-hour period of seat and group work, several students asked what they were supposed to do, in spite of the fact that Mr. Ambrose had listed the morning assignments on the chalkboard. Even though he repeatedly pointed out that the assignments were on the chalkboard, students continued to ask what they were to do. After several students turned in papers before they were called for, Mr. Ambrose explained, "Remember that class assignments not finished during seatwork are supposed to be kept until the next day, even if you get them done later in the day, unless I call for them. If you finish the homework during seatwork time, it can be placed in the turn-in box then." Students continued to act confused, not only about when assignments were due, but also about how to do the work.

Mr. Ambrose frequently works at his desk during seatwork time, but he allows students to come up one at a time if they need assistance. They follow this procedure well, although some of the lowest-achieving students seldom come up. Quite a bit of quiet socializing and other off-task activities go on among students whose seats are located away from the teacher.

Mr. Ambrose has ample activities for students. For example, during a recent one-hour segment of time, he gave students a seatwork assignment and then had them take a quiz (students were told to hold their seatwork papers until after the quiz was completed). Also an extra-credit assignment was listed on the board for students who finished this regular work early. As he handed out the quiz and gave instructions, some students continued to work on the seatwork assignment. Later they had to go to Mr. Ambrose to find out the instructions for the test, and several did not have enough time to complete the test. Mr. Ambrose has told students that they must work harder and do their best or their grades will suffer, but this seems to have had an impact only on the most motivated students in the class.

What steps could Mr. Ambrose take to improve the situation in his class?

CASE STUDY 9–3: A SCIENCE LESSON IN A SIXTH-GRADE CLASS

Ms. Lake has been having great difficulty obtaining acceptable or even completed work from many of her sixth-grade students. They never seem to be able to follow instructions or directions, even for assignments in the textbook. Only the most able four or five pupils are actually doing good-quality work. Ms. Lake likes to challenge the students with new ideas in order to stimulate their curiosity and promote independent thinking. While much of the class appears to enjoy her presentations, the students just don't seem to be able to transfer their enthusiasm to their assignments. For example, in a recent science assignment students were supposed to draw pictures illustrating stages in the evolution of birds from reptiles; most students did not perform satisfactorily. The lesson preceding this assignment included the following components. A five-item test covered questions on birds, reptiles, and vertebrates, reviewing some content covered during the preceding week. Students checked their own answers to this test in class and then passed them in. Although it was not a difficult test, most students got three or fewer items correct. After the checking activity, the teacher began a twenty-minute presentation on the possible evolution of birds from reptiles. The following topics were discussed:

The meaning of adaptation, with an example supplied by students.

An example of environmental action in the local community. This topic was introduced by a student, and other students added comments.

The possibility of life on other planets, including a discussion of the number of solar systems in our galaxy.

A consideration of the question of why birds might evolve from reptiles, with a student's answer, "To get away from enemies, they would take to the air," as the only reason given.

The classification system of living organisms: kingdom, phylum, class, order, genus, and species.

At this point in the presentation students were instructed to copy the classification system from the board. Ms. Lake also provided an example of classification, using the lion in the animal kingdom, vertebrate phylum, mammal class, etc. Two similar examples were also presented and listed on the board. The teacher asked if students understood and if they had any questions. No questions were forthcoming, so the teacher gave the assignment of illustrating the stages in the evolution of a reptile to a bird. Students were given twenty-five minutes and told, "Use some color in your picture, make it neat, and use three stages." As was the case with many of the assignments Ms. Lake gave, only a few students completed their work satisfactorily, although most seemed to make an effort to do some drawing, and many students checked frequently with Ms. Lake to see if their pictures were acceptable.

What problems are evident and what changes might Ms. Lake make to achieve more success in helping students complete assignments satisfactorily?

APPENDIX A
FURTHER READINGS
ON CLASSROOM
MANAGEMENT
AND DISCIPLINE

Association for Supervision and Curriculum Development, *Effective Classroom Management for the Elementary School* (Videotape). Alexandria, Va.: Association for Supervision and Curriculum Development, 1981. This half-hour video tape shows excerpts from the first day of school in a very effective teacher's classroom. Many concepts presented in this book are illustrated.

Canter, L., and M. Canter, *Assertive Discipline*. Los Angeles: Lee Canter and Associates, Inc., 1976. The Canters stress that teachers must assert their right to teach in an orderly and disruption-free environment. To accomplish this teachers must establish rules governing classroom conduct and enforce them with a set of clearly defined consequences. A variety of supplementary materials, including video tapes and filmstrips are also available.

Clarizio, H. F., *Toward Positive Classroom Discipline*, 3rd ed. New York: John Wiley and Sons, Inc., 1980. This book represents many applications of the behavioral or learning theory approach to classroom discipline. Much of the book (and the behavior modification literature generally) is focused on techniques for dealing with disruptive behavior and developing more appropriate behaviors. Because of its extensive treatment of reward and punishment, this book is especially appropriate as a supplement for Chapter Four (Rewards and Penalties) and Chapter Six (Maintaining Good Behavior).

Doyle, W., *Classroom Management*. West Lafayette, Ind.: Kappa Delta Pi, P.O. Box A, 1980. This thirty-one-page booklet is a concise and readable summary of major concepts needed to understand the teacher's classroom management tasks. Defining the teacher's immediate task as "to gain and maintain the cooperation of the students in activities that fill classroom time," Doyle examines a variety of factors that influence what teachers do, and he also describes teacher behaviors that contribute to effective management.

Dreikurs, R., B. Grunwald, and F. Pepper, *Maintaining Sanity in the Classroom: Classroom Management Techniques,* 2nd ed. New York: Harper & Row, Publishers, 1982. Dreikurs regards misbehavior as deriving from mistaken goals: seeking attention, power, revenge, or withdrawal. Only when the individual perceives a connection between behavior and its logical and natural consequences will appropriate change take place. Thus, planning the classroom environment so that the students understand the consequences of their behavior is essential to promoting effective discipline. The book contains many suggestions and applications for teachers.

Duke, D., ed., *Classroom Management. The 78th Yearbook of the National Society of Education, Part II*. Chicago: University of Chicago Press, 1979.

Duke, D., ed., *Helping Teachers Manage Classrooms*. Alexandria, Va.: Association for Supervision and Curriculum Development, 1982. The two books edited by Duke are collections of articles reviewing different aspects of classroom management. Some of the book chapters summarize research; others consider more theoretical or conceptual issues. These books will give the reader a thorough overview of the field and will provide many helpful references for following up particular lines of inquiry.

Gazda, G., F. Asbury, F. Balzer, W. Childers, and R. Walters, *Human Relations Development: A Manual for Educators,* 2nd ed. Boston: Allyn & Bacon, 1977. This book emphasizes the teacher's skills in developing interpersonal communication and relationships. Because teachers interact daily with many children or adolescents, their parents, and other adults, they must be able to listen and respond in ways that facilitate understanding, avoid miscommunication, and solve problems. The book contains many exercises to aid the reader in developing such skills.

Glasser, W., A. Bassin, E. Bratter, and R. Rachin, *The Reality Therapy Reader: A Survey of the Work of William Glasser*. New York: Harper & Row Publishers, 1976. Reality therapy is an approach to dealing with individuals to get them to choose more appropriate behavior. Widely used in school settings, this approach involves clearly identifying consequences for student behavior and being sure that the student understands them. Reality therapy probably works best when it is adopted as a schoolwide system of discipline; however, there is much valuable information for the individual teacher who must deal with inappropriate behavior.

Good, T. L., and J. Brophy, *Looking in Classrooms,* 2nd ed. New York: Harper & Row Publishers, 1978. Two good chapters on classroom management in this book make it a valuable source for teachers looking for a readable summary of classroom management applications. Other chapters treat topics related to classroom management such as teacher expectations, modeling, and grouping.

Gordon, T., *Teacher Effectiveness Training*. New York: Peter H. Wyden, 1974. This book emphasizes the teacher's ability to communicate effectively with students. Listening skills and techniques for dealing constructively with students when their misbehavior causes a problem are described. Although Gordon's approach is not a comprehensive management program, it does offer skills that are helpful for talking with students about their behavior.

Kounin, J., *Discipline and Group Management in Classrooms*. New York: Holt, Rinehart & Winston, 1970. This book reports the results of several of Kounin's studies of group management. Along with behavior modification research, it forms the basis for much current thinking about effective management. This book was not intended to be a compendium of suggestions for classroom teachers, but it does provide informative and clear illustrations of key teacher behaviors.

Readers interested in other publications on classroom management by this book's authors can select from the following references.

Clements, B. S., and Evertson, C. M. "Orchestrating Small Group Instruction in Elementary School Classrooms." Austin, Texas: The Research and Development Center for Teacher Education, 1982, Report No. 6053, 34pp.

Emmer, E. T., and Evertson, C. M. "Synthesis of Research on Classroom Management." *Educational Leadership*, 1981, *38*, 342–347.

Emmer, E. T., Evertson, C. M., and Anderson, L. M. "Effective Classroom Management at the Beginning of the School Year." *The Elementary School Journal*, 1980, *80*, 219–231.

Evertson, C. M., and Emmer, E. T. "Effective Management at the Beginning of the School Year in Junior High Classes." *Journal of Educational Psychology*, 1982, *74*, 485–498.

Evertson, C. M. "Differences in Instructional Activities in Higher- and Lower-Achieving Junior High English and Math Classes." *The Elementary School Journal*, 1982, *82*, 329–350.

Evertson, C. M., Emmer, E. T., Clements, B. S., Sanford, J. P., and Worsham, M. E. *Classroom Management for Elementary Teachers*. Englewood Cliffs, N.J.: Prentice-Hall, Inc., 1984.

Evertson, C. M., Emmer, E. T., Sanford, J. P., & Clements, B. S., Improving Classroom Management: An Experiment in Elementary Classrooms, *The Elementary School Journal*, 1983, *84*, (2) in press.

Evertson, C. M., Sanford, J. P., and Emmer, E. T. "Effects of Class Heterogeneity in Junior High School." *American Educational Research Journal*, 1981, *18*, 219–232.

Sanford, J. P., Emmer, E. T., and Clements, B. S. "Improving Classroom Management." *Educational Leadership*, 1983, *40*, 56–61.

APPENDIX B
ANSWER KEYS
FOR CHAPTER ACTIVITIES

Chapter 1: Activity 1

The room arrangement shown in Figure 1-1 could contribute to classroom management problems in a number of ways:

When the teacher presents information to the whole class from the area near the main chalkboard, students on the other side of the room will be quite distant from the chalkboard and the teacher. This will make it difficult for them to see some of the material written on the chalkboard, and it will be more difficult for the teacher to monitor these students. At the same time, the teacher's range of movement is restricted to a relatively small area, and there is no place to store materials needed in whole-group presentations.

Traffic lanes are clogged or blocked, especially near the bookshelves and en route to the bathrooms and the pencil sharpener.

The small-group tables in the center of the room are too near student desks. Not only might the arrangement cause distractions for students seated at their desks, but there is no place at the table where the teacher can sit and easily see everybody in the room.

Because of the location of the bookcase, the center may be difficult to monitor.

Some students have their backs to the chalkboard and to the main presentation area.

When the teacher assists some individual students at their desks, he or she will have difficulty seeing students in several places in the room.

The isolated desk near the girls' restroom door is a source of potential problems. Not only does it block the path to the door, but a student seated at the desk would be distracted by and be a distraction to students coming and going from this area. Also, the location of the desk makes it very difficult for the teacher to monitor a student seated there.

The student sitting at the desk against the teacher's desk might be distracted if the teacher worked with other students at the desk. Also this desk is located far from the main instructional area.

Problem 6–1

Ms. Johnson should review her expectations for student behavior in the problem areas to be sure they are clear, reasonable, and concretely stated. Then at the beginning of class the next day, she should discuss them with the students. The following suggestions might also help improve behavior:

Circulate among the students and monitor the class continuously in order to anticipate and prevent misbehavior before it occurs. Whenever possible, statements about behavior should be work-related and positively stated. For example: "You should be working on problems 6 through 15. All work should be done silently." "*After* you have turned in your assignment, you may read your library book." "If you are having problems with this assignment, raise your hand and I'll come to your desk."

No more than one warning should be given before following through with consequences. Threats and idle warnings undermine credibility.

Stated consequences should be appropriate to the behavior and carried out consistently. Positive consequences for appropriate behavior should also be included in the list of specific consequences. Academic performance and other appropriate classroom behavior should be rewarded regularly. Rewards may include teacher attention and smiles, praise, stars or happy faces, treats, happy notes, privileges, etc.

The teacher should decide what minor inappropriate student behavior can be ignored so that lessons are not constantly interrupted to deal with behavior that is unlikely to persist or cause a problem.

Ms. Johnson needs to make sure the students have enough work to do, that they understand the assignment, and that they know what to do after they finish it. Student papers ought to be examined periodically to be sure students are following directions and are able to do the work

Ms. Johnson should give some thought to whether the children have been given adequate breaks and changes of pace during the day. She might set aside some class time for student movement and activity.

The children who call out inappropriately can be ignored and encouraged to raise their hands. They can be signaled with a finger over the lips or with a hand raised briefly when they call out. Praising or rewarding hand raising and other appropriate participation when it occurs will encourage students to follow correct procedures.

Problem 6–2

Mr. Wilson could use the following strategies to deal with these students:

Jimmy

Check Jimmy's records and, if possible, talk to other teachers who know him to find out if his behavior in Mr. Wilson's class is typical. If not, then his parents can be called or a conference arranged to get at the reasons for Jimmy's poor participation. Other teachers also may have helpful suggestions for encouraging good behavior on his part.

Jimmy's academic skills should be checked to be sure that his behavior is not caused by an inability to do the work. If it is, then adjustments in the assignments and work requirements are called for.

Jimmy should be seated where he can be monitored more easily and away from children who might encourage his out-of-seat behavior. He should also not sit in high-traffic areas where he might be frequently distracted.

At the beginning of each assignment Jimmy should be checked to be sure he has several sharpened pencils and all his materials. He can be reminded when it is all right to go to the pencil sharpener, wastebasket, materials center, and other places until the teacher is certain that he knows what is appropriate and what is not appropriate.

After giving directions the teacher could ask Jimmy to repeat them to be sure he understands each assignment. Then the teacher should stay close to Jimmy to be sure he gets started. Throughout the activity his behavior should be monitored to see that he is progressing satisfactorily on the assignment.

Jimmy can be permitted to earn some movement by completing an assignment without getting out of his seat. He might be allowed to take something to the office or to another teacher, erase or write on one section of the chalkboard, empty the pencil sharpener, etc.

Another positive strategy would be to put a star on each paper completed in one sitting, send a "happy gram" to his parents on good days, or let him carry a note to the office saying he was a "super student" on days when he is cooperative.

Whenever possible break up assignments into parts or reduce the assignments to prevent the possibility of Jimmy's feeling overwhelmed.

Richard

Avoid overracting to Richard's attempts to get attention. Make clear to him what behavior is acceptable and help him formulate a plan for developing more appropriate behavior.

Identify some constructive things that Richard can do to earn recognition (e.g., preparing an oral report for extra credit, raising his hand and waiting to be called on before responding).

Let Richard tell the class a joke or ask a riddle for each specific period of time he does not talk out (e.g., during one discussion period, one lesson, story time). Provide ample opportunity for Richard to participate appropriately in class discussions, and call on him when he does raise his hand. When he contributes or asks an appropriate question, praise him and give him attention for it.

Set specific consequences for speaking out without permission and making inappropriate comments, then carry these out consistently. Consequences for breaking the rules might include such things as having to wait in his seat one minute after the class leaves for recess, sitting in the hall to do his work, spending five or ten minutes of "time out" away from the students, receiving detention, or being sent to the school office after receiving a certain number of demerits.

If Richard's behavior does not improve and he is in an intermediate grade, he can be required to write a contract in which he agrees to practice appropriate behavior and to stop particular misbehaviors. His parents should also be called to discuss his behavior. They may have a suggestion for ways to deal with him or they may be willing to establish a consequence at home for continued misbehavior in your classroom.

If he continues to be uncooperative, Richard can be seated away from other students with his face to the wall, out in the hallway, or behind a screen. The next day, if his behavior is improved, a system can be tried in which he can earn his way back into the class with a full hour of appropriate behavior. He should be allowed to remain with the class only as long as his behavior is in compliance with the classroom rules.

Problem 7–1

The following suggestions for Mr. Hart could improve his students' seatwork performance:

He should make sure everyone understands instructions before starting groups. Explanation alone may not be sufficient; students should be questioned and they should repeat key directions. Mr. Hart can also write the directions on the chalkboard. Students should be told what will be checked and when.

If seatwork includes some silent reading, reading comprehension questions can be listed on the board so that students have a focus for their reading and know what they will be accountable for when they are called to the reading circle.

Students may need help pacing themselves. The teacher can show them on the clock how much time the first assignment should take or set a timer to signal when they should be finished with a particular assignment.

In order to have time to get the seatwork group started, Mr. Hart can give the first reading group a getting-ready task to complete before he joins them. This will enable him to monitor all seatwork students at the beginning of the activity to be sure they have made a good start.

After working with the reading group for a while, the teacher can give these students a short task to do on their own while he checks on the progress of out-of-group students and answers their questions. When out-of-group students are wasting time and in danger of not completing other necessary activities, their papers can be marked in red to show each student's progress on the first assignment. They can then start on their next assignment, but they should be required to finish the first assignment at home or later in class.

Students should not be allowed to interrupt the teacher with questions during small-group instruction. Students should be told to skip troublesome parts until the teacher can talk to them, or student monitors can be assigned the responsibility of giving assistance to children who need it.

A visual signal, such as a sign or a flag, can be used to inform students when they may approach the teacher with questions and when they may not.

A "help" list for the class may be established. Children can sign the list if they want to talk to the teacher when he is busy. The teacher needs to be conscientious about checking the list and going to the children as soon as possible (e.g., between reading groups).

Students need to know what they may and may not do once their assignments have been completed. They should be given free-time enrichment activities or provided with a good set of interesting materials for free reading.

Problem 7–2

The following items would help Ms. Jones improve her students' attention to and comprehension of instruction.

Ms. Jones should make sure she has all students' attention beginning instruction. She should look around the room and check to be sure all students have the correct materials on their desks before proceeding.

If instructions or directions for assignments are at all complex, the lesson should be outlined and activities or assignments subdivided into easier-to-understand parts or steps.

During content development activities, Ms. Jones should obtain frequent work samples by having students do problems or answer questions. She should circulate around the room during these times, checking for areas of confusion, common problems, and students who are not participating. Based on feedback from these work samples, instruction should be adjusted by either slowing down or increasing the pace of the presentation and by repeating material if necessary.

After instructions have been given, students can be asked to repeat the instructions. Instructions can also be summarized on the board.

Students' faces should be carefully observed while giving directions. Signs of confusion and inattention should be used as cues for questioning students and providing further instruction as needed. When getting students ready to work on an assignment, the teacher shows students the proper form for their work unless it is very similar to work they have already done.

Ms. Jones should not go to her desk immediately after giving assignments; instead, she should circulate while students are beginning the work, checking to be sure they are able to do it correctly and that they are using their time wisely.

Students should not be allowed to come up to the teacher's desk for help until everyone has begun work and the teacher is satisfied that she no longer needs to monitor the whole class actively. Then, if students need further help, they should be allowed to come up to the desk one at a time.

Problem 8–1

The following approaches would help the team operate more smoothly.

Strive for good cooperation and group planning among unit or team teachers. Each teacher must try to maintain the schedule. Have students watch the time. Post times for students to leave and list the materials they should take with them. Use a timer if necessary.

Use established routines as much as possible for beginning and ending lessons; monitor the class to be sure students follow them.

Teach students exactly what behaviors are expected during transitions; include expectations for voice level, use of the pencil sharpener, procedures for passing between classes, getting ready for the lesson, and so on.

If early-arriving students are a problem, establish a "waiting area" where these students must wait quietly until the teacher can speak with them without interrupting the class.

Use a short review activity or drill with the class or group while waiting for stragglers to arrive.

Make sure students know what they are supposed to do when they return to the class. If they return while the teacher is conducting a lesson, give the group or the class a brief task to do while making sure students coming in get settled.

Problem 8–2

Following are some specific suggestions for Ms. Ortiz:

Each day, plan assignments that all students can complete, then provide supplementary assignments at different levels: enrichment and extension for faster students, review and practice assignments for slower students.

Find out if any students in the class qualify for special assistance (such as special education resource room or bilingual tutoring).

Use some small-group instruction in both reading and (at least temporarily) in mathematics. Be sure to keep groups flexible, changing membership according to achievement.

Consider whether it might be possible to team with one or more teachers so that students on similar levels can be grouped for basic skills instruction.

Consider the use of peer tutoring for certain activities and assignments.

Share materials with other teachers to build a collection of supplementary materials above and below your grade level.

Arrange student seating so that you have easy access to lower-ability students and can monitor and help them readily during whole-class instruction.

Be sure to include all students in class discussions and recitations. Do not let faster students answer most of the questions.

After giving assignment directions to the whole class, check the lower-ability students first to make sure they understand directions and are beginning work. If more than two or three students need further directions, meet with them immediately as a small group.

When instructing the lower-level students, break assignments and lessons into small segments and check frequently for understanding. Follow the suggestions for basic skill instruction presented in the section on teaching low-ability students in Chapter Eight.

Case Study 9–1

Diagnosis. Ms. Wade has failed to communicate and reinforce her expectations for classroom behavior and to establish rules and procedures that deal with the problem areas in her classroom. She apparently did not stop inappropriate behavior when it first began occurring; as a result, what could have been a good start during the first weeks of school has deteriorated into a difficult situation. At this point even the well-behaved students are misbehaving and her only deterrent has lost its effect.

Suggestions. Ms. Wade should decide what kinds of behavior she expects of her students, both with regard to general conduct as well as procedures they should follow in particular activities. She should then develop new rules and procedures where they are needed and clarify and reteach those that were part of her original plan but are no longer effective. For example, she could set aside specific times for students to get drinks, use the restroom, sharpen pencils, or visit the class pets.

In addition, she should select a time—perhaps a Monday or the day after a school vacation—to introduce or to review and reteach the rules and procedures to her class. She should also explain to the students the rationales for the desired behaviors, and perhaps rehearse complex ones so that she can give students feedback about especially important behaviors. She will certainly want to review with the students when they may whisper quietly and when they must maintain silence. Because students have acquired some poor classroom talk habits, they may need visual cues such as stop or go signs to remind them when they must be silent and when they may whisper or talk in classroom voices. She can also help students learn when it is appropriate to talk quietly and when it is not by alerting them about class noise level and encouraging them to monitor it themselves.

Ms. Wade should review procedures for working in small groups with the students. She may need to adopt the following practices:

Use shorter seatwork periods, breaking up activities in the groups more often.

Help students pace themselves by setting a timer to signal when work should be completed.

Tell students ahead of time what work will be checked and when. Remind them that they will be questioned about their assignment when they come to the reading circle.

Make sure that students in the first group understand their assignment by checking for understanding and having them do an example or two before calling for the second group.

Monitor the out-of-group students for appropriate behavior while working with the reading group.

After sending one group back to seatwork, don't call the second group until the work of the other students has been checked and help given when needed.

Once the rules and procedures are introduced—or reintroduced—to the class, Ms. Wade should:

Monitor the class with the goal of anticipating and preventing misbehavior before it occurs and noting appropriate behavior.

Make sure that students have enough work to do and that they understand and are able to complete tasks. Students should also know what specific things they can do when they have finished their assigned work.

Structure some time for student movement and activity.

Make statements that pace students through their work such as: "You should now be working on problems 2 through 5. No one should be talking," or "After I've checked your paper you may go to the listening center."

Reward academic performance and other desirable classroom behavior regularly, using stars, happy faces, displays of student work, pats on the back, smiles, etc.

Be certain that stated consequences for inappropriate behavior are related to the misbehavior and that they can be carried out consistently. Positive consequences as well as negative ones should be communicated to students.

Case Study 9–2

Diagnosis.   The continuing confusion of Mr. Ambrose's students about due dates, directions, and completion of work suggests that although he may have planned plenty of work for the students, he may not be explaining requirements clearly nor checking for understanding frequently enough. In addition, students are not receiving feedback about their progress or the quality of their work nor are there any apparent rewards or penalties connected with work completion or lack of it. Having students hold papers until the next day may result in many of them being misplaced and in further delay in receiving feedback about the correctness of the work.

Suggestions.   Mr. Ambrose can begin to improve his situation by trying the following strategies:

> Each assignment should be explained carefully and in detail in addition to being posted on the chalkboard. Students could also be encouraged to keep an assignment book or some other record of daily assignments in particular subjects. In addition, Mr. Ambrose could keep a record of the assignments in a folder so that students could refer to it if needed or check on assignments they missed while they were absent. Keeping several days' assignments posted on the chalkboard may be confusing unless these are clearly marked.

> While giving directions and explanations, Mr. Ambrose should be aware of signs of confusion or inattention. He should also be sure to go over sample questions, problems, or exercises with the class, use a standard format for student headings on papers, and use routines whenever possible to avoid constantly having to reexplain or give new directions.

> Mr. Ambrose should also have students begin assignments under his direction. He can do a small part of the assignment orally, then question students to check their understanding until he is sure they can work independently.

> He should circulate around the class and monitor student progress rather than sit at his desk doing paper work. He should allow students to come to his desk for help only after they have tried the assignment. Then he should allow only one student at a time to come up. When several students need help, he should circulate around the class again, rather than encouraging "come-ups."

> Assignments should be checked and collected as they are completed. If they are too complex to be checked immediately, Mr. Ambrose should check for completeness and return incomplete work to the students to finish. It may be helpful to set aside one or two specific times each day to review each student's progress on their assignments. That way students will know they are accountable, and Mr. Ambrose can more easily identify problems that students are having with work. In addition he will be able to identify students who are having difficulty and need extra help

before they get too far behind. Students who fail to turn in assignments should be given assistance and direction promptly.

Students can be encouraged to set goals by helping them keep records of their scores on assignments in particular subjects. Mr. Ambrose may be able to boost motivation by encouraging the students to set a class goal of improved completion rates or overall student averages, and then provide a treat or a special activity as a reward.

Case Study 9–3

Diagnosis.   Although Ms. Lake has planned interesting presentations, her students seem to be floundering during the follow-up activities. A large part of Ms. Lake's problem lies with poor instructional clarity, poor sequencing of activities, and unclear directions. Students' poor showing on the five-item test suggests that related content from the previous week had not been understood. The twenty-minute presentation contains several indicators of poor clarity, including presenting information out of sequence, backtracking, inserting extraneous information, and moving from one topic to another without warning. In addition, the assignment does not support the content development activity. The assignment is made without checking for understanding and the directions are vague and indefinite.

Suggestions.   Ms. Lake would achieve more success with her class if she concentrated on the following items:

> Information should be presented systematically; plan the lesson sequence and stick to it; state major goals and objectives; pace the lesson so that adequate time is available to cover major points; and avoid vagueness by being specific and using familiar words.

> Ms. Lake should review her procedures for keeping students responsible for work, especially in the areas of communicating work requirements and giving directions clearly. She should be sure that step-by-step directions are given for complex assignments, and she should ask students to repeat directions if there is a possibility that they do not understand them.

> During content development activities, frequent work samples should be obtained and other checks on student comprehension used. With this information, available instruction can be adjusted as needed.

> The amount of information being presented in any one lesson should be considered carefully. It might be better to present less information and leave sufficient time to check classwork prior to assigning students homework.

> Complex lessons should be broken down into smaller parts and later concepts should not be presented until primary ones are mastered.

If some students still do not seem to understand after a presentation and discussion, the teacher can meet with them in a small group to review the presentation and answer questions. If one or two students consistently have difficulty, they can be seated near the teacher's desk so that it is easier to work with them.

During the seatwork portion of lessons, the teacher should circulate to check student progress and to make sure that assignment directions are being followed.

INDEX

A